MAVERICKS
STAMPEDE

Dirk Leads Dallas to the 2011 NBA Championship

» ROB MAHONEY

TRIUMPH
BOOKS

This book is available in quantity at special discounts for your group or organization.
For further information, contact:

Triumph Books
542 South Dearborn Street
Suite 750
Chicago, Illinois 60605
(312) 939–3330
Fax (312) 663–3557

www.triumphbooks.com

Printed in U.S.A.
ISBN: 978-1-60078-685-3

Content packaged by Mojo Media, Inc.
Joe Funk: Editor
Jason Hinman: Creative Director

Interior photos courtesy of AP Images

Cover photos courtesy of Getty Images

Contents

Introduction

After the buzzer sounded, ending Game 6 of the 2011 NBA Finals, Dirk Nowitzki climbed off of the court at the American Airlines Arena as quickly as he could. He paced through the arena's tunnels to the Dallas Mavericks locker room, overwhelmed by the entirety of an incredible moment he had imagined so many times before, but had never been able to clutch as his own.

These precious few minutes belonged to him, and in the privacy of the locker room, Nowitzki held his own emotional celebration, a joyous cleansing after a career's worth of setbacks and obstacles. Every difficulty had been wiped away, and the star who had a decade's worth of criticism ringing in his ears would soon have a ring of his own in response.

He had done it, but more importantly, *they* had done it. The Dallas Mavericks, a true team in every sense of the word, had thrived in every situation in which they were supposed to crumble. The strength of their opposition mattered little; whether facing off with the Trail Blazers in the first round or the Heat in the NBA Finals, the Mavs retained their eternal calm, that guide by which they were able to so easily preserve a system and an ideal. Their commitment to that system was pressured and tested, but Dallas never wavered. They found the open man. They scrambled defensively. They managed to create a coordinated and transcendent whole from a group of mismatched parts, and overcame everything that got in their way.

It wasn't easy, but it never is—not for any champion, no matter how simple their path may seem. Dallas dismissed the Los Angeles Lakers—fresh off their own back-to-back titles—in just four games in the second round, but the emotional investment in a series of that magnitude is considerable, regardless of its length. Every step and every game is a challenge, and that's to say nothing about the hardships Dallas faced during the regular season. The Mavericks somehow lost Caron Butler for the season and Rodrigue Beaubois for most of the season—not to mention Dirk Nowitzki for about a month—and still managed to pull off a breathtaking run to secure their ultimate goal.

Regardless of what stood in their path—be it the absence of a starter or a 15-point fourth-quarter deficit—Mavericks head coach Rick Carlisle preached to the value of process. Whether in terms of an entire season, a game, or even a single possession, it all comes down to that process—to the ability to create something of worth in a team that goes deeper than just winning or losing. These Dallas Mavericks targeted specific goals, stayed true to the system, and looked to improve over the long-term rather than rely on quick fixes. They worked and prepared tirelessly, and when they were finally in a position to capitalize on all of their efforts, they played brilliant basketball in four consecutive playoff series, conquered public doubt, and stole the NBA title from the hands of the Miami Heat. ▪

Game 1
Miami Heat 92
Dallas Mavericks 84

The Mavericks and Heat began the 2011 NBA Finals in the unavoidable shadow of their 2006 encounter; even with Dirk Nowitzki, Jason Terry, Dwyane Wade, and Udonis Haslem as the only holdovers, the 2006 subplot had become such a dominant narrative point of the 2011 championship round that no player or coach could avoid it. That series has become such an important part of both teams' identities that anything more—even a collision between one of the league's most prolific offenses and one of its most oppressive defenses— was deemed little more than a rematch.

Nowitzki and Terry had no intention of letting this series torment them as that one did, but only Nowitzki played well enough in Game 1 make that a reality. JET struggled from the field, in part because he suffered from the inconvenience of having an off night on the NBA's biggest stage, but also due to the fact that Erik Spoelstra had wisely switched LeBron James onto Terry during the fourth quarter. Terry only connected on 30 percent of his shots, and couldn't give Dallas the firepower it needed to keep up with the likes of James, Wade, and Chris Bosh, who scored a combined 65 points in the slow-paced opening affair.

Still, the foundation was there for the Mavericks' to improve, if only because of their uncharacteristically poor start on the offensive end. The Heat accomplished plenty with their fast-footed defense, but Nowitzki's missed layups, J.J. Barea's botched runners, and Terry's poor decisions gave Dallas

Dirk Nowitzki and the Mavericks knew they were in for a battle when they faced Miami's vaunted Big Three of LeBron James, Dwyane Wade, and Chris Bosh.

such little margin for error. Credit Miami's D for the way they challenged shots—and even for the impact of their potential challenges, which clearly had Barea shaking in his boots—but, the Mavericks were capable of playing much, much better.

Shawn Marion and DeShawn Stevenson had some success in man-to-man coverage against LeBron James and Dwyane Wade, but it didn't last. Dallas eventually transitioned into zone coverage and then back to man-to-man, with that final switch bringing their downfall. James and Wade did as they willed against flawed man defense, combining to shoot 6-of-9 from three-point range.

Defending Wade and James is always predicated on concession in some form. Teams often cede long jumpers to James and Wade in the hopes that it lures two of the league's best creators off the dribble into taking decidedly less efficient shots and stalling their team's offense in the process. That's still a semi-effective strategy against Wade (particularly due to his poor shooting from three-point range), but James had somehow become even more un-guardable by hitting threes with consistency throughout the post-season. Oh, how things would change between that night and the one that decided the series almost two weeks later, in which James would be painted as a scape-goat for all of Miami's shortcomings.

The Mavericks, oddly enough, could rest well knowing they still had their best games to come. Dallas' struggles went past those of Nowitzki, Terry, or Barea. Offensive rebounding was a significant problem in Game 1, but one that could be remedied with a better team-wide effort to keep the Heat off the glass in Game 2. Otherwise, all the Mavericks needed to do was continue to execute and endure the Heat's runs; the resilience of Dallas' players and system had paid off in every series thus far, and even though Miami presented the greatest challenge yet, they were beatable, still. ∎

J.J. Barea defends LeBron James during the first half of Game 1 of the NBA Finals on May 31, 2011, in Miami.

Game 2
Dallas Mavericks 95
Miami Heat 93

Somehow, the 2011 Dallas Mavericks were able to treat every fourth-quarter deficit with the sense of urgency it deserved without overdoing things. Even with the clock on their backs, they didn't rush shots. They didn't allow the defense to dictate anything. They just executed the sets as effectively as they would at any other point in the game, and put their best scorers in the best position possible to go to work.

In most cases that means getting the ball to Dirk Nowitzki on the wing or in the high post, and spacing the floor perfectly in order to prevent an easy double team. That's precisely what the Mavericks did with less than 10 seconds remaining in Game 2, as Dirk Nowitzki worked to the left side of the floor, spun past Chris Bosh, and finished an amazing layup—while sporting a splint to protect a torn tendon in his left hand, no less—to put the Mavs up by two after climbing out of a 15-point fourth quarter deficit. This is just what the Mavs do. We—as observers of the game—love to lionize clutch performances, but there's something inherently pedestrian about the way Dallas goes about their business at the end of games. They don't rise to the occasion, but maintain their even keel. This team is fearless. They know they possess the ability to out-execute any other squad in the league. Shawn Marion knows that if LeBron James somehow gets by him, then the pressure will be there. Jason Kidd knows that if he positions himself perfectly on the perimeter, then Nowitzki will be able to hit him with a kick-out pass from the post. Jason Terry knows that if he makes hard cuts

Dirk Nowitzki aims at the basket as the Heat's Udonis Haslem and Chris Bosh defend during the last minutes of the second half of Game 2 of the NBA Finals on June 2, 2011. The Mavericks defeated the Heat 95–93.

and curls, that his teammates will reward him with the ball in his spots. These aren't beliefs, but facts, solidified elements confirmed by actual events.

For any other club, a win like this would represent incredible fortitude. For Dallas, it's just another comeback in a line of great comebacks, albeit their most significant yet. They excel at making feats of extraordinary strength appear natural, to a degree that even the demolition of a 15-point Heat lead in the fourth quarter somehow seems commonplace.

The Mavericks don't have the kind of athletic talent that makes highlight reel dunks look easy, but the way they move the ball and find shooters is not, on any level, normal. Dallas has a truly exemplary offense, and yet you'd never know it as Jason Kidd makes a relatively routine pass to the corner at just the right time, or Tyson Chandler sets a barely legal screen to free up Dirk Nowitzki with enough room to launch an off-balance jumper. Nothing in their equation is ordinary, and yet it's all instinctive, all reactive, all a product of a team filled with intelligent ball players doing merely what they know to do.

Seven minutes—the amount of time it took for Dallas to wipe away that 15-point deficit—is a long time to contend with an offense like that, even for an elite defense like Miami. The Heat D is fast and flexible, but nonetheless subject to the mandates of the offense. When Dirk touched the ball, Miami was largely forced to double. When the ball swung this way or that, the Heat were forced to shift to compensate. All of this is a fundamental part of the offense-defense dynamic, but when the free-wheeling Mavs dictated everything with their crisp passing and perfect spacing, the Heat could only do so much.

Dallas had done their job in stealing one of the first two games on the road, but their three-game home stand would not be easy. History hasn't favored the team forced to defend their home court for three straight games in the NBA Finals, but Dallas would have to do their best to maintain whatever edge they had created with their remarkable comeback. ▪

Shawn Marion and Tyson Chandler battle for a Game 2 rebound with the Heat's LeBron James, Udonis Haslem, and Chris Bosh.

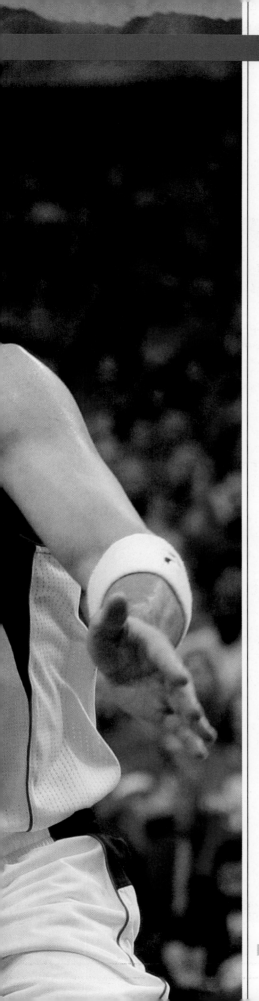

Game 3
Miami Heat 88
Dallas Mavericks 86

If Game 2 served as a reminder of all that the Mavericks are capable of, Game 3 offered a bitter counterpoint concerning the fine line between success and failure. Dallas had to do so much right just to be in a position to win Game 2, and when they fed Dirk Nowitzki for one final possession, his layup fell and all was right with the world.

Dallas worked just as hard to remain competitive in Game 3 in response to some considerable pressure from the Heat, but with the game hanging in the balance, Nowitzki committed a costly turnover on one possession and barely missed a potential game-tying shot as the buzzer sounded. The heroes of the clutch, it seems, were not infallible.

Yet as much as we'd like to pretend that games and series rely on those moments that come with the clock ticking toward zero, in reality they're decided by an incredible combination of factors. Nowitzki may have missed a makeable shot that could have sent the game to overtime, but that's not the reason Dallas lost. The Mavericks lost because Dwyane Wade had an incredible 29-point, 11-rebound performance. They lost because Mario Chalmers oozed confidence from every pore, and made four of his six three-point attempts. They lost because LeBron James was able to find his teammates despite not being able to score particularly well. They lost because the two primary ball-handlers, Jason Kidd and J.J. Barea, committed four turnovers apiece. All of these setbacks blossomed into an immensely difficult set of circumstances, one that even the Mavericks' uncanny knack for comebacks couldn't overcome.

Dwyane Wade tries to turn the corner on Jason Kidd during the first half of Game 3 of the NBA Finals on June 5, 2011, in Dallas.

Maybe it's fitting then that the Mavs' rally hardly seemed like their usual comeback formula, even though they once trailed by 13 points. All Dallas did was play, and though they spotted Miami points here and there by way of their own errors, it's not as if the Mavs were horrid, even at their worst. The difference between the bumbling Mavs and those blazing the comeback trail was actually fairly thin; hitting the defensive glass and taking care of the ball was all it took for Dallas to give themselves a chance in this game, and so would be the case for the remainder of the series.

The micro and macro battles between Dallas' offense and Miami's defense were absolutely phenomenal, but the other end of the court deserves its due; the Mavs played terrific team defense against LeBron James, and though Dwyane Wade wasn't hindered in the same way, slowing the MVP enough to create a balanced series was a significant accomplishment. Dallas—specifically Tyson Chandler, Shawn Marion, and Dirk Nowitzki (yes, Dirk Nowitzki)—completely halted Miami's pick-and-roll execution in Games 2 and 3, taking away an invaluable element of the Heat's half-court offense. The Mavericks may not have been an elite defensive team throughout the regular season or the first three rounds of the playoffs, but their scrambling man and zone coverages were working wonders against the best player the NBA had to offer.

Even that defensive excellence couldn't take the Mavs quite as far as they needed to go. Only two of Nowitzki's teammates were able to score in double figures, and though Shawn Marion had been a tremendous offensive contributor in the first two games of the series, his performance slipped a bit in Game 3. Dallas had a typically brilliant Nowitzki night and some success getting to the foul line as their offensive foundation, but nothing was built upon it; even with their eventual comeback pulling things to a virtual draw, the Mavs weren't playing quite well enough offensively to warrant an outright victory. ■

LeBron James, once again using his left arm to bar-off a defender, drives during the second half of Game 3 against Shawn Marion.

Game 4

Dallas Mavericks 86
Miami Heat 83

The unfortunate thing about the prevalent NBA narrative is almost obsessive need for comparison. The singularity of every event is damned for the sake of creating an analogue, as if it were some impossibility for a player to stand on his own two feet without being propped up by the past.

Dirk Nowitzki played Game 4 of the NBA Finals while suffering from a sinus infection, but this wasn't Michael Jordan's unforgettable "flu game" (Game 5 of the 1997 NBA Finals). This was one of the game's truly unique stars trudging through his own story with its own definitions. Irrelevant of the fact that Nowitzki didn't even approach Jordan's production when ill (MJ somehow managed to score 38 against the Jazz that night, despite appearing ready to collapse at any moment), we should know better than to use all of the goings-on in this basketball world as an excuse to abuse our ability to recall. Not every player who suits up while ill is Michael, just as every star who returns from injury mid-game isn't Willis Reed.

Nowitzki didn't have his "flu game," but he did play in Game 4 to the best of his ability. He struggled with his shot despite finding some good looks, and yet managed to bounce back and score 10 points in the fourth quarter—more than Dwyane Wade, LeBron James, and Chris Bosh combined. Nowitzki was again the anchor for another impressive comeback; this time, his points fueled the 17–4 run the Mavs used to erase a nine-point fourth quarter deficit. A performance like that—even as a part of a 6-of-19 night—needs no boost from a slight resemblance to events from more than a decade ago.

LeBron James and Tyson Chandler battle for a rebound during Game 4 of the NBA Finals on June 7, 2011. The Mavericks won the game 86–83 to tie the series at 2–2.

Then again, maybe it's best that Nowitzki's illness take a narrative backseat. Rick Carlisle pulled off some rotation magic in Game 4 that deserves center-stage treatment. Peja Stojakovic had proven to be too much of a defensive liability to be played significant minutes in this series, but with Caron Butler still recovering from injury and Rodrigue Beaubois inactive, Carlisle's options were limited.

Instead, Carlisle threw J.J. Barea into the starting lineup, and moved DeShawn Stevenson behind Shawn Marion in the rotation. Marion had been forced to play incredibly heavy minutes as a result of Stojakovic's defensive limitations, but by moving Barea into the starting lineup and Stevenson to the bench, Carlisle would have the means to rest Marion when necessary while adding a ball-handler to open games. Each of those three Mavs involved in the rotation switch responded with their best games of the series.

Not only had Carlisle done a fantastic job of balancing a micro-managing style with the release of control (when he lets the Mavs "just play basketball") in the Finals, he had pressed the right buttons in every single series of the 2011 postseason. Starting Barea as a means to eliminate Stojakovic from the rotation was actually rather inspired, and though Barea hadn't played particularly well in the first three games of the Finals, he was able to add another dimension to the Mavs' starting offense with his dribble penetration.

Dallas continued their remarkable defense against LeBron James, who was somehow held to just eight points on 3-of-11 shooting with four turnovers. Though James did manage nine rebounds and seven assists, his impact was quashed. Dallas had completely taken James out of the game by pressuring him at every turn, a strategy in which Tyson Chandler was absolutely crucial. Any payoff that the Mavs had already received in acquiring Chandler had paid off ten-fold in the Finals. Dallas had yet to come up with a true answer for Dwyane Wade (who followed up his stellar performance in Game 3 by scoring 32 points on just 20 shots), but with James locked down, Carlisle making all the right moves, and Nowitzki closing out games, Wade's impact was trumped. ■

Tyson Chandler fist bumps with a Mavericks fan after Dallas' Game 4 victory.

Game 5
Dallas Mavericks 112
Miami Heat 103

Dallas had managed to respond after each of their losses and kept Miami from establishing any momentum. But Game 5 was pivotal—whichever team broke the 2–2 tie with a victory had a significantly better chance of taking the NBA title, and the Mavericks could take care of business on their home court. They delivered with the most impressive offensive performance by any team in the Finals: an incredible shooting display executed within the NBA's most fantastically structured offense.

The Mavericks shot a ridiculous 13-of-19 from three-point range in Game 5, thanks to the exceptional accuracy of Jason Kidd, Jason Terry, and J.J. Barea. All three had open looks created through the flow of the offense, but they also connected on tough, contested threes that no player has any business making. The Mavericks hit their tough shots and their easy shots, and completely overwhelmed a Heat offense that performed quite well by any other standard save for the game's final margin.

Much was made of LeBron James' alleged disappearance in this series, but he managed to put together a decent performance in Game 5. The Finals just aren't a stage conducive to decent performances, and more is expected of a player of James' talents. It's not absurd to expect James to be the best player on the floor, and from that perspective—the one he's created

Tyson Chandler blocks a shot by the Heat's Chris Bosh in Game 5 on June 9, 2011, in Dallas. The Mavericks won 112–103 to take a 3–2 lead in the series.

by, frankly, being the best player in every other setting but this one—James surely disappointed. Still, lost in the nationwide LeBron shaming was the impact of a Dallas defense that was prepared to counter him.

On a related note: James was correct in his postgame assessment of the Heat's performance. Miami played well enough to win this game, they just didn't have the defensive means to counter Dallas' incredible shooting. The Heat's defense was unquestionably their weaker link. Defensive breakdowns led to open Tyson Chandler dunks, wide-open three-pointers, open driving lanes for Barea to attack, and some oddly open opportunities for Nowitzki (who scored 29 points on 50 percent shooting). The Mavs' accuracy—even in the face of good defensive pressure—may have put them over the top, but it was those breakdowns in coverage leading to shots around the rim that really doomed the Heat.

One more win. That's all that stood between the Mavericks and the prize they were never supposed to capture, between Dirk Nowitzki and the validation that players like him supposedly—if you buy into that brand of ridiculous criticism—didn't have in them to secure. There was still so much left to be accomplished—stealing another game in Miami would be no easy feat—but Dallas' versatility and perseverance gave them reason for optimism. Rick Carlisle and his staff would iron out the wrinkles and have the Mavs ready to roll. The title still eluded the Mavericks, but they would be prepared to close in Miami. ■

Jason Terry and Dirk Nowitzki celebrate after winning Game 5 of the NBA Finals.

Game 6
Dallas Mavericks 105
Miami Heat 95

In fitting fashion, the Mavericks had to dig deep into their rotation to close out the series. With Brendan Haywood sidelined by a hip injury, Brian Cardinal and Ian Mahinmi were asked to contribute. Both filled valuable minutes in Haywood's stead, and though neither player threatened to become a rotation regular for next season, they managed to score a combined seven points. DeShawn Stevenson also came off the bench to hit a trio of three-pointers and provide some rest for Shawn Marion.

Those 18 points could very well have been the difference between securing the Mavericks' first-ever title and having to play in a potentially devastating Game 7. Stevenson, Cardinal, and Mahinmi hit back-breaking buckets that either killed Heat runs or extended Maverick scoring spurts.

As tempting as it is to shift the focus on Dirk Nowitzki or those working in the background, the true star of the clinching game was Jason Terry. Terry scored 27 points on incredible 11-of-16 shooting to finish off the Heat, the kind of playoffs performance often missing in the past. JET was a juggernaut in Game 6, and though it would have been particularly apt for Nowitzki to end the series with a massive performance, he'll have to settle for scoring 10 points on eight shots in the fourth quarter. It's unlikely that Nowitzki's shooting struggles every crossed his mind once that final buzzer sounded.

The offense swelled, and the defense held. Dallas pulled off a complete performance in the 2011 NBA Finals and, for that matter, throughout the

Dirk Nowitzki drives past Chris Bosh in Game 6 of the NBA Finals on June 12, 2011, in Miami.

2011 playoffs. Their offense and defense weren't always clicking in concert, but Dallas managed to sustain their efforts on both ends with a collective effectiveness. When the offense hit a snag, the defense tightened up, and when the defense became problematic, the offense shifted into high gear. It's not easy to construct a team that's this capable of performing at an elite level on both ends of the court, but Mark Cuban and Donnie Nelson built a champion.

They traded for Jason Kidd to steady the half-court offense and orchestrate in the clutch. They re-signed Dirk Nowitzki, without whom the franchise would be lost. They extended Jason Terry, despite faulty public concerns over his fit with the team. They signed Shawn Marion and Brendan Haywood to ill-advised, lucrative deals that worked out better than anyone could have imagined. They unearthed J.J. Barea, whose wizardry off the dribble was one of the many highlights of a phenomenal playoff run. They acquired Caron Butler, who cannot be forgotten even though he watched the postseason from the sidelines. They found bit players to fill out the roster, several of whom provided a lift when Dallas needed it most. They took all of these pieces, this group that has but one true superstar and a team full of support, and thanks to the efforts of Rick Carlisle and his staff, made it into one of the most remarkable championship teams in NBA history.

It wasn't easy, and it certainly wasn't cheap. But this was the championship that Mavericks fans deserved. It was a fitting tribute to the hard work of a crew of veterans, none of whom had previously felt the sting in their eyes from showers of champagne. It validated players, it changed legacies, and it affirmed a system. The Larry O'Brien trophy didn't change anything about the fundamental fiber of those players or that system; it doesn't make Nowitzki or the Mavericks organization any greater than they already were. But it does make them new, and it does bring them peace. For once, Dirk Nowitzki, as a new man, can rest easy knowing all that he's dreamed of finally belongs to him. He is unconquerable. Unimpeachable. He's an NBA champion, and no one can ever take that away from him. ■

Dirk Nowitzki, Jason Kidd, and Jason Terry hold up their trophies after Game 6 of the NBA Finals against the Miami Heat Sunday, June 12, 2011, in Miami. The Mavericks won 105–95 to win the series and the NBA championship.

2010–2011

Mavericks: What's Old Is New

The 2010–2011 Dallas Mavericks were not championship favorites—not at the beginning of the regular season, the start of the postseason, or at any particular point in between or beyond. They had neither the incredible size of the reigning champion Los Angeles Lakers nor the talent of the newly formed Miami Heat.

They didn't have the pedigree of the San Antonio Spurs or the defensive intensity of the Boston Celtics. What's worse: almost every one of the Mavs' core players began the season with the prime of their careers in the rear-view mirror. These Dallas Mavericks were a collection of skilled and capable veterans, but there were compelling reasons to believe in their basketball mortality, if only because the NBA landscape was filled with teams of seemingly superior potential.

Yet even with all of that in mind, the Mavericks began the season with an unmistakable hope. Media Day was filled with the usual promises of a successful campaign to come, but players like Dirk Nowitzki, Shawn Marion, and Tyson Chandler projected a pure confidence; the Maverick players spoke of a championship not because it was expected of them as athletes in a preseason setting, but because they each held such tremendous confidence in the players assembled that a title seemed like a perfectly reasonable expectation.

Dirk Nowitzki and Brendan Haywood celebrate during an early-season game. The Mavericks' unique chemistry helped them form one of the most close-knit units in the league.

Dallas began their season with a 7–2 sprint, and it was easy to see from where that confidence stemmed. Though the core of the team had remained fundamentally the same from the year prior—the Mavericks' only significant off-season acquisition was Tyson Chandler, who had played just 51 games the year prior for the Charlotte Bobcats thanks to lingering injury problems—their defensive execution was unmistakably improved. It's not uncommon for skilled offensive teams to begin a new year preaching the virtues of defense, but the Dallas Mavericks lived out that virtue from the opening day of the 2010–2011 season. Rick Carlisle's defensive system had given the Mavs an effective defense in years past, but Chandler's intelligence, athleticism, and leadership took that system to an entirely new level.

Dallas had traded away their previous starting center, Erick Dampier, in order to acquire Chandler, and stylistically, the two players could hardly be more different. Dampier's strong, burly frame helped him to stave off opponents in the low post, but also limited his mobility, and thus his ability to defend the pick-and-roll. It's not enough for a center to merely be big; those on the back line of an NBA defense require the agility to defend against opposing guards coming off of a screen, and while Dampier was reasonably effective in curtailing

(opposite) Caron Butler drives to the basket. A midseason acquisition in 2010, Butler was expected to play a key role on the 2010–11 Mavericks. Though he averaged 15 points per game, Butler's year was cut short after he underwent knee surgery in January. (above) One of the best bench players in the NBA, Jason Terry has seen his role evolve throughout his seven seasons in Dallas. Known for his outgoing personality, Terry has adjusted to his changing roles with ease.

Dirk Nowitzki shares a smile with self-described sidekick Jason Terry. The lone holdovers from the Maverick team that lost the NBA Finals to Miami in 2006, the two veterans saw 2011 as an opportunity to get the ring they had been denied five years earlier.

the pick-and-roll action of Maverick opponents, he was a player defined by his limitations. Dampier had become a punchline of sorts among NBA fans due to the gaudy size of his contract and all that he couldn't do on the court, and while those jabs were perhaps unfair, there was some truth in the notion that Dampier was far from an ideal defensive center.

Chandler was immediately able to do what Dampier was not, as his quick feet and long arms allowed him to pressure opposing ball-handlers and contest shots at the rim at almost every turn. He was an omnipresent defender, seemingly able to impact every stage of a defensive possession. Plus, his demeanor was entirely different from Dampier's in a way that was beneficial to the team defense; gone was the stoic, big-bodied center of the past, replaced by the active and communicative center of the present and hopefully, the future. Chandler's on-court communication allowed him to function as a true defensive anchor, the value of which the Mavericks benefited from immediately.

With defenders like Shawn Marion and Jason Kidd on the perimeter and scorers like Dirk Nowitzki, Jason Terry, and Caron Butler in the fold, Dallas had a chance to create true balance in their performance on both ends of the court. That two-way success guided them to a 24–7 record through the end of the calendar year, with big wins over Miami, Oklahoma City, San Antonio, Boston, and a number of other future playoff teams. The Mavericks may not have been championship favorites, but they made quick work of most of their early regular season opponents by way of newfound defensive success.

A Season on the Rails

Any momentum that the Mavericks gained over the first few months of the season was halted on the first day of 2011. In the first quarter of a game against the Milwaukee Bucks, Caron Butler launched upward in an attempt to secure an offensive rebound, but returned to the floor in a crumpled heap, clutching his right knee. Butler writhed in pain, pounding on the floor, perhaps already all too aware of the dreadful news that would come through media reports over the next few days.

A slew of tests confirmed what many team officials had feared: In all likelihood, Butler's season was finished. He had torn the patellar tendon in his right knee, and even the slightest possibility of a return to the court would require a ridiculously optimistic recovery timeline, painful, diligent rehab work from Butler, and a great deal of luck. Dallas had little option but to grow accustomed to life without their starting shooting guard, a tall order even for a team as impressively deep as the Mavericks.

Season-ending injuries each come with their own sense of tragedy, but Butler's freak, non-contact tear was especially unfortunate considering how effective he had been for the Mavs this season. Butler had only been a Maverick since the trade deadline of the 2009–2010 campaign, but he had grown considerably since his arrival in Dallas. Butler had been featured prominently on offense throughout his career with the Washington Wizards, but his offensive role in Dallas was to be quite different; Dirk Nowitzki has been the focal point of the Maverick offense for more than a decade, and rather than function as a go-to scorer in isolation, Butler was slated to be a complementary piece, working off the ball along with Jason Terry and Shawn Marion.

That fact had seemed lost on Butler initially, as he frequently stopped the flow of the offense during his initial half-season with the Mavs. Butler is, and has always been, a capable scorer, but his tendency to halt the team's ball movement created significant problems for Dallas in last season's playoffs. Butler's talent may have suggested a capability for a greater impact, but his performance on the floor appeared incongruent with the fluid, versatile

Caron Butler drives against the Milwaukee Bucks on New Year's Day before going down with a season-ending knee injury later in the game. Also without Dirk Nowitzki, the Mavericks lost 99-87.

attack the Mavs hoped to employ.

Butler entered the 2010–2011 season a new man. He had slimmed down considerably after a busy off-season spent working out with legendary trainer Tim Grover, and he spoke of having a more comfortable feel for his place in the Mavs' offense. It's never easy for a player to pick up and fully understand an entirely new playbook following a midseason trade, but after having several months to review Dallas' sets and work with the coaching staff, Butler seemed prepared to reinvent his game as a Maverick.

The change in Butler's game was immediately noticeable. Although his production actually dropped slightly in comparison to the season prior (Butler averaged 15.2 points and 5.4 rebounds per game as a Maverick in 2009–2010, and 15.0 points and 4.1 rebounds per game in 2010–2011), Butler was actually shooting far more efficiently from the field and keeping his numbers up despite playing fewer minutes. He had indeed found his comfort zone, and in his efforts to better fit in with his Maverick teammates, Butler worked on becoming a more aggressive driver and a better perimeter shooter. His vastly improved three-point range gave Dallas another excellent complement to Nowitzki as well as a release option when opposing defenses chose to attack Dirk with double teams.

Just as importantly, Butler had

(opposite) Caron Butler goes hard to the basket against Minnesota defender Kevin Love. After Butler went down with a season-ending knee injury in January, the Mavericks dedicated their 2011 playoff run to the veteran forward. (above) Jason Terry and Caron Butler celebrate after the final buzzer of the Mavericks' win over the Phoenix Suns on December 17, 2010. The two combined for 35 points in the 106–91 victory.

J.J. Barea goes hard to the basket for two of his nine points against the Indiana Pacers on January 12. Playing without Dirk Nowitzki, the Mavericks lost their third straight game, 102–89.

evolved into a crucial component of the Mavs' defense. Shawn Marion may have been Dallas' de facto defensive stopper, but Butler was quietly the superior wing defender during the regular season. His ability to guard the likes of Dwyane Wade, Kevin Durant, and Manu Ginobili was invaluable, and while the instant reaction to Butler's injury from fans and media members may have focused on the loss of a scoring threat, it was that capability to lock down on defense that the Mavs would miss most.

The impact of Butler's injury was compounded by the fact that Nowitzki had just missed his third straight game with a knee injury of his own, and would go on to miss seven more. The Mavs were left to make do without two of their most important players, and though the remaining players competed throughout Nowitzki's absence, Dallas is uniquely incapable without the presence and influence of its star player. It's not even a matter of talent; the Mavericks have capable pieces, but they only fit in a way that makes sense when Nowitzki is at the focus. Nowitzki is the element that gives the team its on-court synergy, and while removing him from the equation doesn't make Kidd lose his playmaking acumen or Terry a lesser shooter, it does botch the spacing and flow to which the Mavs had grown accustomed.

The Mavs proceeded to lose six consecutive games, with the final two losses in that stretch coming even after Nowitzki's return. Dallas was officially in a rut; a six-game losing streak represented the monumental drop-off that the Mavs had experienced since their injury troubles, and the fact that the losses continued even with Nowitzki back in the lineup painted a dismal image of the months to come. After all, if Dallas was having such a hard time coping without Butler in January, how would they fare in April?

Expectations, Misfortune, and Rodrigue Beaubois

Though Butler's injury cast an undeniable cloud over the Mavericks franchise, there still remained one great hope. Rodrigue Beaubois, the second-year guard from the French archipelago of Guadeloupe, was finally nearing the end of his recovery from an off-season foot injury. Beaubois had followed up his impressive rookie year with a summer playing for the French national team, but unfortunately broke a bone in his foot during a practice in preparation for the 2010 FIBA World Championships. Beaubois was at one point rumored to be looking at a return to the court during the preseason, but the preseason came and went without the Mavs' only dynamic young scorer playing a single minute.

So went the entire process of Beaubois' rehabilitation; he was rumored for a return on opening night, then in December, and then in January, but all three of those marks came and went without Beaubois suiting up.

Beaubois' prolonged recovery was made even more painful by the unquestionable anticipation that surrounded his sophomore season. Beaubois had been the Mavs' best per-minute scorer behind Nowitzki during his rookie year, but his minutes were limited. That didn't stop Beaubois from shining in his moments on the floor—he dropped 40 against the Golden State Warriors in a 2009–2010 regular season game—but Rick Carlisle still held the keys to the rotation and opted to keep Beaubois locked out. That decision sparked a bit of controversy in the 2010 playoffs, when Carlisle finally opted to play Beaubois in a potential elimination game against the San Antonio Spurs. Beaubois immediately ignited the Mavs' offense with his speed and shooting, but was benched for most of the fourth quarter in favor of Jason Terry. Terry was awful, and the Mavs were eliminated from the playoffs in a close, hard-fought game.

Struggling with knee pain at the time, Dirk Nowitzki shoots before the Mavericks' January 12 game against the Pacers in Indianapolis. The Mavericks offense simply did not flow well without its star as Dallas lost four straight without Nowitzki.

Beaubois' second year in the NBA was supposed to be different, but his chance to play serious minutes was delayed due to lingering foot problems. Once those health issues finally subsided, Beaubois was thrown into the mix. Carlisle still didn't play Beaubois heavy minutes, but that was more of a product of Beaubois oddly inefficient play and the depth of the team than any miscalculation on the part of Carlisle.

Things just weren't the same for Beaubois after returning from injury. He oscillated between extremes of passivity and over-aggressiveness, never able to find the happy medium that had guided his play during the previous season. Beaubois was even gifted minutes on occasion, but all of that playing time couldn't boost Beaubois back to his rookie levels of scoring and efficiency. His shooting percentages dropped and his turnovers jumped; the offensive contributions of an offense-first guard were

suddenly in question, and though Beaubois was thought to be the heir apparent to Butler's position and minutes, he never quite played as if he was worthy of the gig. Most NBA players have their struggles at some point or another, and Beaubois unfortunately had his in a moment when the Mavs sorely needed his contributions.

This time around, Carlisle tried to keep Beaubois in the rotation for as long as he could, but by the time the regular season had come to a close, DeShawn Stevenson had taken over the starting shooting guard slot and Beaubois had faded into the background.

Dallas went on to have a miraculous season, but their journey wasn't without its own hardships. Beaubois is still only valuable in the hope he provides for next season, despite the fact that he was supposed to be a significant contributor this season. Butler's injury cast Dallas in an entirely different light, and offered a reminder of

(opposite) Rodrigue Beaubois' quick first step allows him to get to the rim faster than perhaps any Dallas teammate. Though he faded into the background as the 2010–2011 season came to an end, expectations are still high for the guard from France. (above) Beaubois battles the Clippers' Blake Griffin for a loose ball during Dallas' April 8 win over Los Angeles. Beaubois was scoreless in 25 minutes.

how fragile team success really is. Nowitzki's minor injury troubles ushered in a problematic stretch for an otherwise wildly successful Maverick team, and when the Mavericks were unable to fully rebound from that lull, their statistical outlook took a significant hit. Dallas had once looked like an elite team, but by season's end their inconsistency had caused such problems that they were merely very good on both offense and defense rather than top notch. Being sub-elite is a pretty nice problem to have, all things considered, but it was still a notable step down from the heights Dallas had once climbed to, and a rather significant obstacle in the Mavericks' pursuit of their lofty playoff aspirations.

That said, the elite Mavs were still there, merely obscured by the team's occasionally underwhelming alter ego. Dallas wasn't able to perform at a high level during every game, but inconsistency shouldn't be confused with inability. At the top of their game, the Mavs were able to contend with anyone. Their performance in the season's first few months was no fluke, and though Butler's performance was valuable, his loss wasn't completely damning. The Mavs could get by without Butler, and considering the circumstances and the goals the team had established at the beginning of the season, they'd have to. ∎

(opposite) After a quiet 2009–10 season in Charlotte, Tyson Chandler resurrected his career in Dallas. The big man shot a career-high 65 percent from the field during the regular season, started all 74 games he played in, and averaged 10.1 points per game. (above) Shawn Marion battles through the Lakers' defense.

The Mavericks defend against the Sacramento Kings' Omri Casspi during Dallas' 116–110 win on February 16. Rodrigue Beaubois made his season debut in the win, scoring 13 points in 21 minutes.

Game 1
Dallas Mavericks 89
Portland Trail Blazers 81

The first-round match-up between the Dallas Mavericks and Portland Trail-blazers was predicted to be a close series of mostly offsetting mismatches, and the first game of the series unfolded accordingly. Dirk Nowitzki scored 28 points on 20 shots to go along with 10 rebounds against some impressive defense from LaMarcus Aldridge and Nicolas Batum. Aldridge himself scored both inside and out en route to a 27-point, six-rebound night. Both players were defended relatively well, but neither could be deterred.

However, with Nowitzki and Aldridge playing to a virtual draw, Game 1 was tilted by a bit of a wild card. Jason Kidd uncharacteristically hunted for scoring opportunities from the game's opening possession, and finished with 24 points—impressive considering the slow pace of the game, but borderline unimaginable when factoring in the source of the points—by hitting a ridiculous six of 10 attempts from beyond the arc. Kidd's perimeter shooting provided a downright dominant scoring presence, but even with that unexpected scoring surge, the Blazers had put themselves in a position to win this game.

It was then that fans were introduced to what would become the central theme of the Mavericks' playoff run. Nowitzki scored 16 invaluable fourth quarter points—including 12 straight—by repeatedly drawing fouls and getting to the free throw line, and Dallas managed to erase Portland's six-point fourth quarter lead. Aldridge, Andre Miller, and Nicolas Batum had scored well, but Nowitzki's free throws allowed the Mavs to swing the game with quick and efficient scoring.

Ultimately, Dallas took a strong night from Aldridge and kept moving. They kept working to execute their offense, and though defending Aldridge seemed to be a lost cause, they did what they could to limit Portland's peripheral scorers. Gerald Wallace was active, but seemed phased out; his drives lacked resolve, and his activity on the court didn't translate into any tangible benefit. Four of Wallace's nine missed field goals were blocked attempts.

With Wallace and Brandon Roy negated, the Mavs were able to make up for lackluster offensive nights by Jason Terry, Shawn Marion, and J.J. Barea. Dallas still benefited from their bit contributions, but Kidd and Nowitzki were the unquestionable leaders of the effort—the alpha and the omega, as it were. What Kidd started Nowitzki finished, and Dallas was on its way with a victory in opening game of their playoff run. ■

Though Jason Kidd has never been known as a player to look for his own scoring opportunities over distributing the ball, he played his hot hand well in Game 1 against Portland. Including an impressive six three-pointers, Kidd scored 24 points in the tightly defended game.

Game 2
Dallas Mavericks 101
Portland Trail Blazers 89

Though the Mavericks played well against the Blazers in Game 1, there were a few areas of concern. After all, the Mavs needed the aid of an incredible shooting night from Jason Kidd and the foul-drawing talents of Dirk Nowitzki to muster the offense needed to secure a victory, while the Blazers established La-Marcus Aldridge in his comfort zones and worked their bigger guards against the likes of Jason Terry and J.J. Barea in the post.

The possibility was certainly there for a turn in the series, because it was rather unlikely that the Mavs would be able to pull off a victory working within the same set of factors.

So Nowitzki kept drawing fouls and attacking late in the game, Kidd kept making his threes, and the Mavs got a huge night from Peja Stojakovic, to boot. Unsustainability be damned, the Mavs won by taking the same basic formula and widening their success to other areas as well.

Game 2 was marked by the Mavericks' truly pristine performance. Dallas performed well in virtually every area—they drained their shots, corrected their early defensive troubles, kept their turnovers down for the second straight game, maintained a scoring balance that allowed for some fantastic offensive synergy, hit the glass, and got to the line frequently. It's hard for any team to counter such a holistically excellent performance, and though the Blazers were technically within a reasonable striking distance at various points throughout the game, they were dispatched by Nowitzki and company with relative ease.

So much of the Mavs' success (and potential for future success) depended on three-point shooting accuracy, but Dallas' strong shooting was no fluke. The Mavs work hard to get those open looks from the perimeter, and possessions and possessions worth of beautiful ball movement resulted in quality looks from the outside. That Dallas converted on those opportunities was no surprise, and the trend would continue throughout the rest of the playoffs.

This loss was disheartening for Portland, particularly because virtually every Blazer played relatively well. Aldridge was dominant for stretches and efficient overall. Andre Miller hit a few jumpers and got to the rim off the dribble while running the offense effectively. Nicolas Batum and Wesley Matthews hit their shots. Wallace chipped in with his dynamic slashing. Yet none of it was enough.

Plus, Aldridge actually defended Nowitzki quite well, and yet Dirk still managed to put up 33 points while getting the shots that he wanted. Some forces in this universe are simply not meant to be limited or halted, and this particular performance was evidence of Nowitzki at his most elemental. ■

Peja Stojakovic turned back the clock in Game 2, tying his career playoff high with five three-pointers and scoring 21 points.

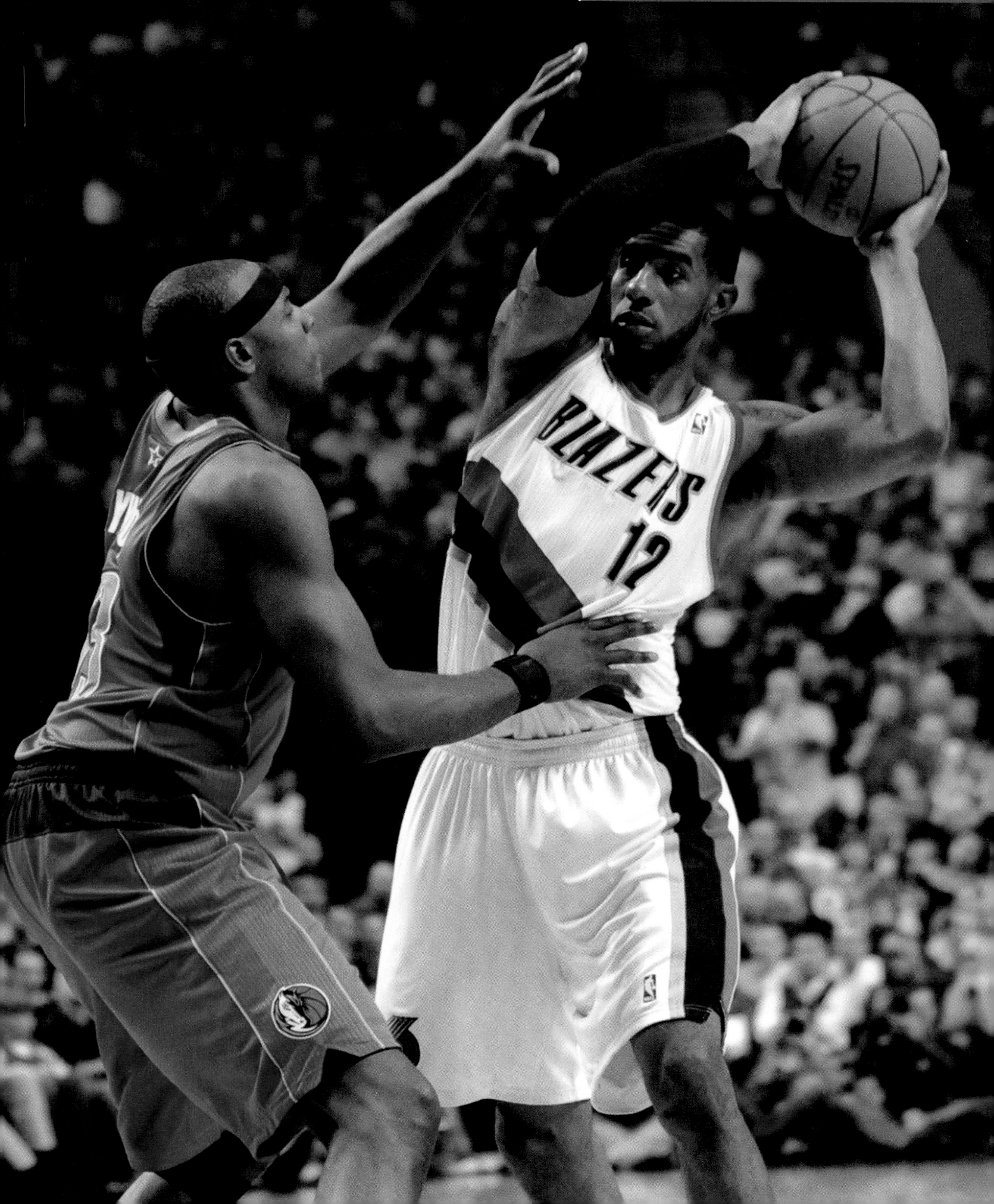
BLAZERS
12

Game 3
Portland Trail Blazers 97
Dallas Mavericks 92

In Game 3, the Dallas Mavericks frittered away possessions with mishandled passes and botched catches. They left points at the free throw line in a game decided by a pretty thin margin. They held the very possibility of a commanding 3–0 lead in their hands, but allowed it to slip through their fingers.

It was a damn shame, too, because for a night, Jason Terry walked on air. JET had played productive minutes in both Games 1 and 2, but his performance in Game 3 was something otherworldly. Terry connected on 10 of 13 shots, including five of seven from three-point range. He was the Mavs' one consistent source of points, and he expertly used his defensive draw to set up teammates for easy scores. Terry was able to fuel Maverick runs and keep the team afloat when the offense struggled, but the Mavs gave up too much to JET's positional counterparts and committed too many turnovers.

Wesley Matthews—who scored 25 points on 12 shots—and Brandon Roy—who had 16 points and four assists—were both fantastic for Portland, and together they accounted for more than half of the Blazers' points. The Mavs just weren't ready to deal with that kind of firepower from the wings, and their defensive shortcomings led to their first loss of the postseason.

That said, the Mavs made visible progress in their defense on LaMarcus Aldridge, who was held to a far more manageable 20 points on 42 percent shooting from the field. Brendan Haywood and Tyson Chandler did incredible individual defensive work against Aldridge, and though the Portland forward hit some crucial shots down the stretch, a few big baskets don't erase Aldridge's less efficient overall line. He may have scored a bit and even kept Chandler off the court by putting him in foul trouble, but his presence was significantly less taxing on the Dallas defense than it had been in games past. At the time it may have seemed like an aberration, but the Mavs' interior defense had a legitimate breakthrough in their losing effort, a slightest hint of their ability to hold strong defensively for the remainder of the series—and the remainder of the playoffs. ■

Brendan Haywood plays tight on LaMarcus Aldridge during Game 3. Though he was quiet on the offensive end, Haywood's defense against Portland's star big man helped keep the Mavericks close.

Jason Kidd blows past Wesley Matthews late in Game 4. The Blazers erased a 23-point deficit to even the series 2–2.

Western Conference Quarterfinals

Conference Semifinals

Game 3
Portland Trail Blazers 97
Dallas Mavericks 92

In Game 3, the Dallas Mavericks frittered away possessions with mishandled passes and botched catches. They left points at the free throw line in a game decided by a pretty thin margin. They held the very possibility of a commanding 3–0 lead in their hands, but allowed it to slip through their fingers.

It was a damn shame, too, because for a night, Jason Terry walked on air. JET had played productive minutes in both Games 1 and 2, but his performance in Game 3 was something otherworldly. Terry connected on 10 of 13 shots, including five of seven from three-point range. He was the Mavs' one consistent source of points, and he expertly used his defensive draw to set up teammates for easy scores. Terry was able to fuel Maverick runs and keep the team afloat when the offense struggled, but the Mavs gave up too much to JET's positional counterparts and committed too many turnovers.

Wesley Matthews—who scored 25 points on 12 shots—and Brandon Roy—who had 16 points and four assists—were both fantastic for Portland, and together they accounted for more than half of the Blazers' points. The Mavs just weren't ready to deal with that kind of firepower from the wings, and their defensive shortcomings led to their first loss of the postseason.

That said, the Mavs made visible progress in their defense on LaMarcus Aldridge, who was held to a far more manageable 20 points on 42 percent shooting from the field. Brendan Haywood and Tyson Chandler did incredible individual defensive work against Aldridge, and though the Portland forward hit some crucial shots down the stretch, a few big baskets don't erase Aldridge's less efficient overall line. He may have scored a bit and even kept Chandler off the court by putting him in foul trouble, but his presence was significantly less taxing on the Dallas defense than it had been in games past. At the time it may have seemed like an aberration, but the Mavs' interior defense had a legitimate breakthrough in their losing effort, a slightest hint of their ability to hold strong defensively for the remainder of the series—and the remainder of the playoffs. ◼

Brendan Haywood plays tight on LaMarcus Aldridge during Game 3. Though he was quiet on the offensive end, Haywood's defense against Portland's star big man helped keep the Mavericks close.

Game 4
Portland Trail Blazers 84
Dallas Mavericks 82

Even though the Mavericks dominated the narrative of the 2011 postseason, there are some elements of that story that do not belong to them. Game 4 was a detour away from the tale of how the Mavericks defied the odds, and an emotional, amazing sidebar look into the world of a forgotten star.

One could see traces of the inevitable Blazers comeback at the end of the third, but the fourth quarter itself contained most of Portland's—and Brandon Roy's—incredible run. Roy turned the entire game (and balanced the series at two wins apiece) off the dribble; the man without knees managed to drive past Jason Kidd, Shawn Marion, and DeShawn Stevenson to score and dish to his heart's delight, and no Mavericks defender could possibly stop him. Not on this night. Not in front of that thunderous Rose Garden crowd. Not in his one transcendent moment, when the entire basketball world rested in the slur of his crossover.

Roy was supposedly finished. He wasn't supposed to be capable of such an outpouring in any game, much less one of this magnitude. Yet there was nothing but truth in Roy's fourth quarter showing (he had 18 points and four assists in that frame alone). The Mavs were forced to grapple with the departure from logic that the situation entailed, but the outcome was unmistakable; a defeated man, who had publicly complained about his lack of play-

ing time just days earlier, was in true superstar form once again, willing his team to victory. Roy's moment may have been fleeting, but it came at a vital time and kept the Blazers' season alive.

The Mavs undoubtedly left Portland wondering what could have been. After coughing up a very winnable Game 3, Dallas concluded Game 4 by surrendering a 23-point second half advantage in most implosive fashion. Dallas' otherwise brilliant offense came sputtering to a halt, as each of the Mavs' most reliable scorers buckled.

The series was merely brought back to square one with Portland's amazing comeback, but Dallas had been in position for a proper close out. There were more opportunities still (and two more games to be played in the comfort of American Airlines Center) but the sense of squandered opportunity was inescapable. At this point, the Mavs could only hope that the seize in their offense wouldn't come back to haunt them, and that Roy's explosion would be seen as we see it now: an amazing performance in a winning game, but ultimately a component in a losing series. ■

Jason Kidd blows past Wesley Matthews late in Game 4. The Blazers erased a 23-point deficit to even the series 2–2.

Game 5
Dallas Mavericks 93
Portland Trail Blazers 82

Tyson Chandler is a man with a loud game, but he had been held to a whisper over the first four contests of this series. No more. In a pivotal Game 5, Chandler exploded into a dominant force, recharging the Mavericks and filling up the box score in the process.

Chandler shifted into overdrive on the offensive glass, where he grabbed an unfathomable 13 offensive boards. That was four more than the Trail Blazers mustered as an entire team, which stands as a testament to Chandler's incredible effort. He found the weak spots in the Blazers rebounding front and exploited them, and helped the Mavs secure a series-high 42 percent of their misses. Dallas' offense wasn't in a very good rhythm (Jason Kidd and J.J. Barea combined to shoot 3-of-13 from the field, while even Dirk Nowitzki and Jason Terry shot less than 50 percent), but Tyson salvaged everything. He scrapped together the remnants of wasted possessions, and converted them into field goals or free throws—a simple act of effort that saved the Mavericks' offense and helped Dallas take a 3–2 series lead.

This was the complete Tyson Chandler experience—elite defense, fantastic rebounding, and engaged offense—something unfelt and unseen in the first four games of this series due to foul trouble, a lack of emphasis on establishing Chandler as an offensive option, and Chandler's own occasional complacency.

For a player who had largely been invisible on the offensive end, this was the way to make an entrance. Chandler had been crucial for the Mavs all season long, and his heralded work on the defensive end (which he continued in Game 5 by holding LaMarcus Aldridge to just 12 points) had only constituted part of his success. So much of Chandler's value lies in what he does for the Mavs' offensively, and though his efforts in Game 5 were more focused on attacking the glass than helping Dallas to space the floor by providing hard rolls to the rim, he nonetheless boosted the Mavs' offensive efficiency and pulled them within one win of the second round.

The Mavericks built their lead through defense and balanced scoring (both of which were tied to Chandler's performance, but also linked to the ubiquitous impact of Jason Kidd), and on this night, they were able to maintain that lead. There were no heroic comebacks this time, no unscripted diversions into Brandon Roy's own made-for-TV movie. When all of the magic of Game 4 had faded, Dallas was left standing as the better team, out-hustling and out-executing Portland at every turn. ◼

All smiles after the final seconds ticked away, J.J. Barea was happy to see the Mavericks escape with a Game 5 win after a tough shooting night.

Game 1
Dallas Mavericks 96
Los Angeles Lakers 94

Dallas had the misfortune—or supposed misfortune, in retrospect—of meeting the defending champion Los Angeles Lakers in the second round of the playoffs. Again, the Mavericks' prospects were filled with doubt; though the Mavs were a capable club, the Lakers' embarrassment of basketball riches seemed to make a Western Conference Finals run by L.A. inevitable.

Still, with a truly unguardable power forward, a deep bench, and two skilled defensive centers to counter Pau Gasol and Andrew Bynum, the Mavericks were uniquely capable of matching up with the Lakers. Even those matchup advantages didn't factor too heavily into the media punditry, though, as the Lakers were almost unanimously predicted to move on to the next round.

The script called for Dallas to fight valiantly, but lose to L.A. in a hard-fought series due to the overwhelming talent of the Lakers core, and Game 1 initially seemed to follow that plot line. The Lakers rattled off a 21–2 run that spanned the second and third quarters to build a 16-point lead, and did so by creating a nice scoring balance and locking down defensively. Kobe Bryant was the game's unquestionable driving force behind the run, and Dallas—like most every other team in the league—lacked a clear means of stopping him.

But these Mavs were nothing if not resilient, and erased nearly every point of their third-quarter deficit with an impressive 20–6 run. Dirk Nowitzki and Tyson Chandler were both fantastic to kick off the second half,

but the surprise story was Corey Brewer, the high-energy forward that the Mavericks acquired midseason through free agency. Brewer's length and motor grant him to the potential to be an elite NBA defender, but the fact that he joined Dallas so late in the season hurt his chances for regular playing time. Rick Carlisle clearly didn't feel comfortable with having Brewer on the floor on a regular basis, but he was willing to inject Brewer's brand of pure hustle into the lineup when the Mavs were looking stagnant.

Brewer's impact was felt immediately. His nine-minute stint was the only court time he would see in the game, but it reversed the night's natural course; Dallas' offense was complemented by an oppressive, scrambling defense, both with and without Brewer in the lineup. The only thing left to do was execute.

Execute the Mavs did. The ball moved beautifully within the offense, and Dallas shot a remarkable 9 of 20 (.450) from three-point range against one of the best three-point defenses in the league. Dallas' ball movement was so crisp, Jason Kidd, Peja Stojakovic, and J.J. Barea

The Lakers' Pau Gasol defends Dirk Nowitzki in Game 1. Nowitzki outscored Gasol 28–15 as Dallas overcame a nine-point halftime deficit to take the series opener.

had time to fire away from outside, and 27 of the Mavs' 96 points came from beyond the arc.

Dallas' flurry of three-pointers made the game a toss-up as time ran down. Both teams were neck and neck for the entirety of the fourth quarter, until two crucial late-game sequences pushed the Mavericks over the top.

On the first, Dallas trailed 94–93 with just 20.3 seconds remaining and was looking to get the ball to Nowitzki for the game's final shot. Gasol fouled Nowitzki from behind in his efforts to get a hand on the inbound pass, and his poor gamble sent Nowitzki to the line for two free throws. Nowitzki, an 89-percent free-throw shooter, calmly sank both to give the Mavs a one-point lead.

On the subsequent play, the Lakers found themselves in a similar situation. Ron Artest inbounded the ball to Gasol, who faced up beyond the three-point line after making the catch. Bryant streaked by Gasol's left side to receive a hand-off, but something went awry. Bryant fell to the floor because of what some thought was a foul on Kidd, but the officiating crew blew no whistle, and Kidd poked away the hand-off attempt and sealed the victory. The two possessions were painful for the Lakers, but the Mavericks earned the victory thanks to superior offensive execution, limiting the Lakers big men, and the high-volume dominance of Nowitzki. It was an unlikely beginning, but the game set the tone for the rest of the series. ▪

(opposite) Tyson Chandler reaches to the rim as Kobe Bryant tries to defend. Chandler finished just short of a double-double with 11 points and nine rebounds. (above) In addition to his 28 points, Dirk Nowitzki was a beast on the boards in Game 1, pulling down a game-high 14 rebounds.

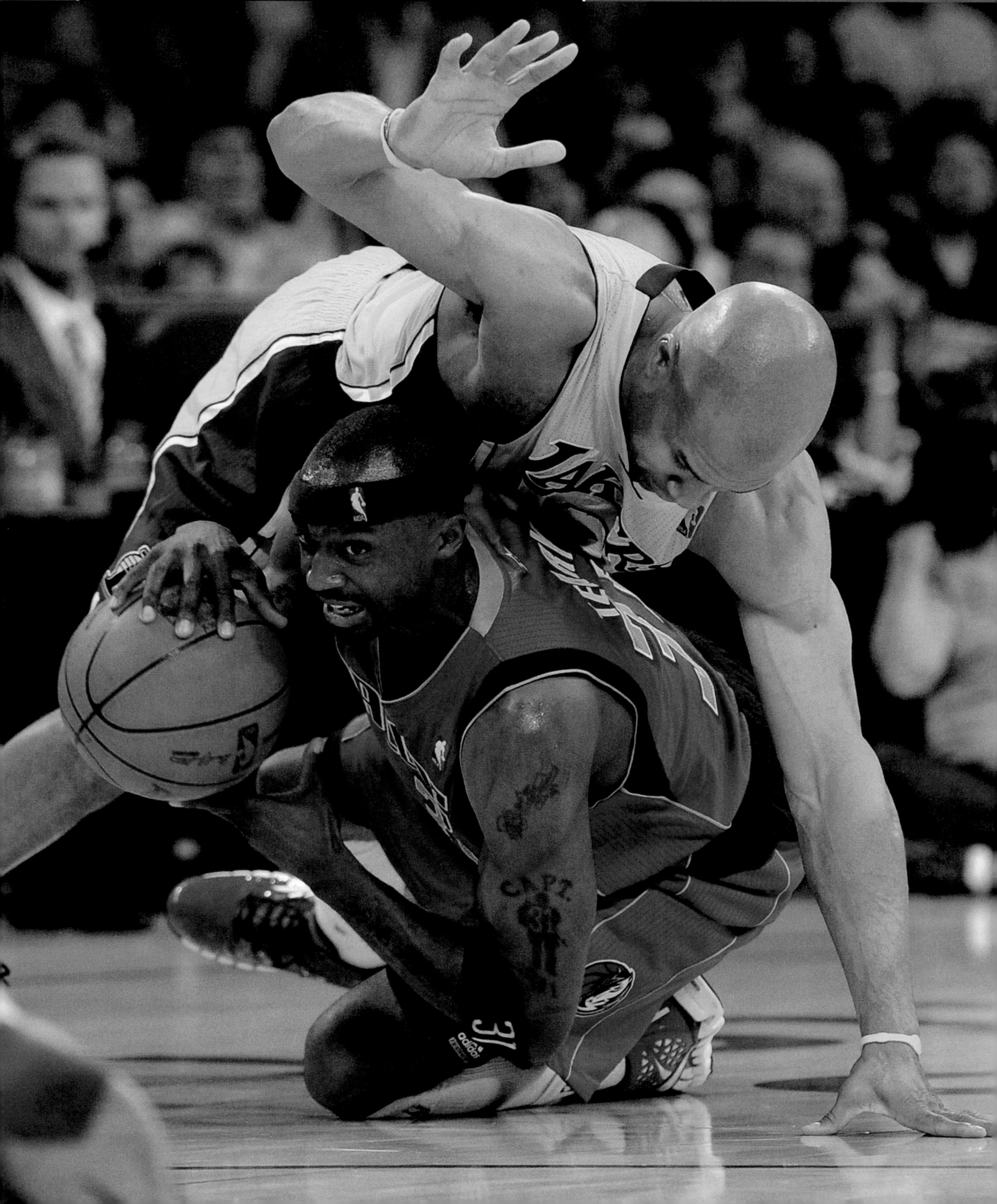

Game 2

Dallas Mavericks 93
Los Angeles Lakers 81

The Mavericks knew they could expect to see a refocused Laker team in Game 2, but apparently the Lakers weren't quite prepared for the fact that the Mavs' Game 1 effort—even in victory—was substandard. Neither team played their best basketball in the first game of the series, but in a vital Game 2, it was the Mavs who stepped up their quality of play.

Dallas wasn't quite as effective from beyond the arc (8 of 25, .320) as they were in Game 1, but they compensated for that by hitting the offensive glass. Shawn Marion and Brendan Haywood each finished the game with four offensive rebounds apiece, and though the boards were supposedly a point of significant Laker advantage, the Mavs were able to make the rebounding margin a non-factor.

The Mavs played some terrific defense, but the Lakers also dug their own grave with poor perimeter shooting; L.A. shot just 2 of 20 on three-pointers (.100), with Kobe Bryant, Steve Blake, and Ron Artest among the most errant gunners. Three-point shooting has never been a significant part of the Laker offense, but that low of a percentage on that many attempts is a brutal drag on any team's offensive efficiency. The Lakers were able to get decent games from Bryant, Andrew Bynum, and Pau Gasol, but with all of those wasted three-point attempts, the Lakers couldn't match the Mavs' incredibly balanced attack.

Nine players suited up for Dallas in Game 2, and every one of them scored at least four points. Dirk Nowitzki was as great as would have been expected, and further

proved that the Lakers have no player capable of matching up with him. Shawn Marion was engaged offensively for the second consecutive game, which is always a good predictor of the Mavs' offensive success; having shooters like Jason Terry or Peja Stojakovic dialed in is one thing, but Marion's slashing, rebounding, and defense provide a dimension that no other Mav can fully replicate. J.J. Barea had his first great game (with others to come), as he tore apart the Laker defense by running high pick-and-roll action with Nowitzki.

Defensively, the Lakers had no answers—not for Dirk, not for Barea, and not for the Mavericks' ball movement. Los Angeles' mental breakdowns were unbelievable for a team with their success and pedigree.

"It's deeply rooted at this point. It's obvious that we have trust issues, individually," Bynum said following Game 2. "All 13 of our guys have trust issues right now. I think it's quite obvious to anyone watching the game—hesitation on passes, and defensively we're not being a good teammate because he wasn't there for you before—little things. And unless we come out and discuss them,

Jason Terry hits the floor as he beats Derek Fisher for a loose ball. The Mavericks' bench made a huge difference in Game 2, outscoring their Laker counterparts 40–12.

nothing is going to change."

Many media outlets heard "trust issues," and ran with it, but Bynum's post-game complaint was much less tabloid-worthy than it seemed. The Lakers clearly did have trust issues; their defensive rotations were nonexistent, and NBA teams are incapable of playing proper defense without the trust that keeps the system together. The Lakers may have had an insane amount of talent, but their on-court synergy—particularly on the defensive end—was inexplicably abysmal.

It's hard to explain exactly why Los Angeles seemed to implode, but Dallas deserved credit for prodding them to that point. The Mavs put sustained pressure on the Lakers with their offense, and each blown rotation by Los Angeles led to only more and more exasperation.

The Lakers could sense their own vulnerability. That much was evident in their miscues and their body language, and was crystallized in Ron Artest's bizarre flagrant foul on J.J. Barea with just 24.4 seconds remaining and the game already decided. The rest of the Lakers didn't respond in such volatile fashion, but their frustration was palpable. Down 2–0, the Lakers were a team on the brink, and while underestimating the defending champs seemed unwise, the Mavs' brutal effectiveness had followers of the game discussing a possible sweep before either team had even touched down in Dallas. ■

(opposite) Dirk Nowitzki shoots his signature fallaway jumper over Lamar Odom. Nowitzki led all scorers with 24 points.
(above) Brendan Haywood skies for two of his five points off the bench.

Game 3
Dallas Mavericks 98
Los Angeles Lakers 92

Dallas' offense in Game 2 may have been defined by balance, but the Game 3 offense was an exhibition of singular brilliance. Dirk Nowitzki drove around Pau Gasol. He shot over the outstretched arms of Lamar Odom. He spun and faked and jab stepped to his heart's delight, and completely eviscerated every defensive strategy the Lakers threw at him. Nowitzki finished with 32 points on just 19 shots—an incredibly efficient outing, even by his lofty standards—and helped push the Mavs' to 5–0, 7–0, and 6–0 bursts in the fourth quarter to grab Dallas' third victory of the series.

Beyond Nowitzki, the Mavs were aided offensively by their ability to get to the free-throw line (Tyson Chandler attempted seven free throws and Jason Terry went to the line eight times) and create new possessions with offensive rebounds. The stats and totals from Game 3 don't seem particularly gaudy, but make no mistake: this was a battle of two highly efficient offenses working each other over, albeit at a slower pace. Transition opportunities were uncommon, but both the Mavs and Lakers were able to get the shot attempts their respective offenses sought to create.

Dallas executed relentlessly on offense. The Lakers' blown pick-and-roll coverage, their inability to cover the corners after a swing pass, and their confusion in rotation are all specific byproducts of the Mavs pressing the right buttons to make the Laker defense squirm. Jason Terry, Jason Kidd, and J.J. Barea generated problems for the Lakers by making smart decisions with the ball, and the Lakers were behind every step of the way. Dallas' power came in the extra pass; that final swing, kick-out, or dump-down broke the Lakers' backs, and it undoubtedly offered Rick Carlisle some sweet relief to see his team working through every possession while the opponents shared looks of growing irritation and defeat.

The Lakers offense actually performed well in Game 3—even well enough to win—but without a player who could even hope to defend Nowitzki much less contain the Mavericks offense, L.A.'s efforts were sunk.

Plus, Dallas just had better timing; the Mavs outscored the Lakers by 12 points in the fourth quarter and finished the game on an upswing. In a game as close as this one, that timing made all the difference, and while that fact may downplay the outright superiority that a 3–0

Beating Lamar Odom to the ball, Tyson Chandler pulls down one of his six rebounds in Game 3.

series advantage suggests, it's only fair that the Lakers are assessed fairly in their performance. Los Angeles could have had Game 3, just as they could have had Game 1. The timing of their runs just didn't coincide with the final minutes of the fourth quarter.

Pau Gasol continued in his underwhelming performance by scoring just 12 points on 5-of-13 (.385) shooting, an unacceptable mark for the Lakers' second-best player. Gasol typically provides Los Angeles with an incredibly potent offensive weapon, but a combination of passivity and the Maverick defense limited his effectiveness. Kobe Bryant, Lamar Odom (who started in the place of a suspended Ron Artest, a product of Artest's cheap flagrant foul at the end of Game 2), and Andrew Bynum helped compensate for Gasol's floundering with efficient scoring performances, but the Lakers couldn't quite match the Mavs' point production.

This was the game that truly turned the series and propelled the Mavericks onward to the Western Conference Finals. There was still basketball to be played, and a chance—however slight—of a Lakers comeback, but by this point the Mavs had effectively won. The back-to-back NBA Champions were hanging their heads, and all that was left to accomplish in this series was the formality of a proper dismissal. ■

(opposite) Jason Terry rises to fire a three-pointer from the corner. Terry made a pair of shots from long range and contributed 23 points off the bench. (above) Hoisting three fingers in the air, Dirk Nowitzki celebrates one of his four three-pointers. Nowitzki led all scorers with 32 points.

Game 4
Dallas Mavericks 122
Los Angeles Lakers 86

The final game of the second-round series between the Dallas Mavericks and Los Angeles Lakers was less a game than a dissection; Dallas picked apart L.A.'s defense with a downright surgical precision, each dagger three-pointer provided a targeted incision, and by game's end, the Lakers had been dissected so exactly that all that remained was the smell of formaldehyde.

The Mavericks' accuracy from the field would be considered unbelievable if the entire affair hadn't been documented on camera and broadcast on national television. According to Kevin Pelton of *Basketball Prospectus,* Dallas' shooting performance in Game 4—as measured by effective field goal percentage, a measure that combines weighted percentages from two and three-point range—was the best of any playoff team in two decades. The Mavs turned a potential closeout game into an all-timer with their ridiculously effective accuracy, and the idea that Jason Terry and Peja Stojakovic could combine to shoot 15-of-16 from beyond the arc while J.J. Barea completed nine of his 14 field goal attempts and Dirk Nowitzki finished seven of his 11 attempts is absurd. It's bonkers, really, especially when considering the level of competition and the desperation that the Lakers were thought to have had.

It was all possible because of the Mavs' endlessly beautiful ball movement. Dallas did an incredible job of finding open space and making the right passes throughout this series. The Lakers embarrassed themselves in Game 4 with their inability to stick with the Mavs' shooters, but they were only put in a position to fail because the passing was so crisp and the cuts were so perfect.

The second and fourth quarters were particularly potent bursts for the Mavs; Dallas scored 72 points (and outscored L.A. by 32 points) in those two quarters combined, due to a variety of contributors. Terry finished with 32 points, and tied an NBA playoff record with nine made three-pointers. Barea dropped 22 of his own, as he continued to run circles around L.A.'s bigs. Stojakovic, who quietly contributed throughout the series, chipped in 21 points and made all six of his three-pointers. Dallas' bench alone managed to score 86 points, matching Los Angeles' overall point total.

Dallas' defense wasn't anything to scoff at, either. Some of the same lethargy that plagued L.A. on the defensive end crept into their offensive game, but it's not as if shots went up unchallenged or passes deflected themselves. The

Shawn Marion goes up for a shot as Ron Artest—fresh off suspension—defends. Marion scored eight points and grabbed six rebounds in 24 minutes.

Mavs were true defensive aggressors, and forced the Lakers into a turnover on nearly a fifth of their possessions while altering a vast majority of their attempts from the field. The duo of Tyson Chandler and Brendan Haywood held Andrew Bynum to just six points and Pau Gasol to a mere 10. Kobe Bryant was able to mount a successful first quarter run, but that short burst was an isolated incident. The Lakers had no continuity, and no consistent scorers.

To make matters worse, Bynum and Lamar Odom lost their composure down the stretch, and each committed a foolish flagrant foul: Odom gave Nowitzki a body check as the two ran up the floor, and Bynum decked a defenseless, airborne Barea on a late-game drive drive to the basket. Bynum was ejected immediately, and was later hit with a five-game suspension and a $25,000 fine. All in all, those events added to the unfortunate mess that was Phil Jackson's final game with the Lakers. Jackson certainly wasn't faultless in L.A.'s playoff struggles, but he nonetheless deserved a more auspicious exit.

The Mavericks' sweep of the defending champs will go down as one of the most impressive triumphs in franchise history, but for this year's team, it was only a step in a longer journey. Dallas was completely committed to the process, and though the Mavs may have even impressed themselves by the speed and command with which they dispatched the Lakers, their gaze remained forward-focused. ∎

(opposite) Tyson Chandler defends tightly on Kobe Bryant. Bryant led the Lakers with just 17 points on 7-of-18 shooting from the field.
(above) Jason Terry showed why he is one of the best sixth men in the NBA, leading all scorers with 32 points, including nine three-pointers.

Game 1
Dallas Mavericks 121
Oklahoma City Thunder 112

Perfection, thy name is Dirk Nowitzki.

Nowitzki began the Western Conference Finals with an irrefutable assertion of his dominance; he systematically made every opposing defender into a mismatch and completed a performance that would surpass a mortal player's wildest dreams. Nowitzki attempted 15 field goals and 24 free throws in Game 1, and somehow missed just three shots, finishing with 48 points. That's an incomprehensible level of efficiency, made possible only by Nowitzki's ability to tap into the ethereal. How else could one possibly explain the events that unfolded on the floor of the American Airlines Center? Nowitzki is not of this planet, this galaxy, or this realm; he has access to some greater basketball power that the rest of simply cannot understand, a force that carefully guides each impossible shot through the net with a ridiculous ease.

Believe it or not, Nowitzki was actually challenged. Kevin Durant put on a scoring display of his own, and though he couldn't quite match Nowitzki's volume or efficiency, 40 points on 10 of 18 shooting is remarkable output, even for one of the game's finest. On any other night, Durant's incredible production would have been the story, and the ordaining of a young star in the biggest game of his life would have grabbed national headlines. But feats of basketball strength are forever boosted or obscured by the power of context. As extraordinary as Durant's performance was, the fact that it came in a losing effort and was trumped by Nowitzki's superior night will cast a shadow over one of the finest showings of the playoffs.

With both teams' superstars functioning at such a high level, it should come as no surprise that Game 1 was a duel between high-powered offenses. Both teams were even more efficient than the score suggests; accurate shooting from the field and frequent trips to the free throw line go a long way, and both teams began the series with what would be their best offensive performances of the Western Conference Finals.

Nowitzki and Jason Terry were expected sources of efficient scoring, but J.J. Barea was again incredible working off the dribble. He ripped the Thunder to shreds in the pick-and-roll, and finished with a hyper-efficient 21 points on just 12 shots. Oklahoma City could have taken Nowitzki's best shot and still won the game, but the Thunder's universal defensive struggles killed them. The Mavs' top four shot-takers all completed more than 50 percent of their attempts and pushed through to a win by way of dynamic offense. ■

Tyson Chandler gets the Western Conference Finals started by tipping off against Oklahoma City's Serge Ibaka.

Oklahoma City Thunder 106
Dallas Mavericks 100

Lost in Dirk Nowitzki's Game 1 brilliance was the inconvenient fact that Dallas actually defended quite poorly. That weakness caught up with the Mavs in Game 2, as James Harden and Eric Maynor emerged from the bench with some fantastic complementary performances. With Kevin Durant and Russell Westbrook attracting so much of the Mavs' defensive attention, Harden and Maynor were free to create off the bounce as they willed.

Jason Terry and J.J. Barea had particular trouble containing that dribble penetration, but Dallas' defensive problems went well beyond them alone. Tyson Chandler, Dirk Nowitzki, and Brendan Haywood deserve some of the responsibility for breakdowns like those suffered in Games 1 and 2, and their collective faults removed one of the Mavs' true advantages in this matchup. When Dallas defended effectively, they were the superior team in the Western Conference Finals. When they played defense as they did in the first two games of this series, the contests devolved into shootouts—or worse. Dallas can still win under those circumstances, but why lean so heavily on the offense when given the choice to diversify?

Terry and Barea faded a bit, and though Tyson Chandler and Jason Kidd stepped up to provide Dirk Nowitzki with a little scoring help, Dallas came up just short because of their second straight defensive no-show.

Russell Westbrook played with much more control than he did in Game 1, but also played fewer minutes; Maynor's success running the point ushered in a temporary coup of the point guard responsibilities, and though

Westbrook is the more dynamic and productive player, he sat during the game's closing minutes after the Thunder offense began to hiccup. Maynor finished the game well, and the public pseudo debate over both players began: Could the Thunder actually be better with Maynor running the show than Westbrook? The easy answer is an emphatic "no," but playoff storylines are nothing without their villains, and Westbrook had the misfortune of alienating viewers with his sometimes overly aggressive style.

Also, Game 2 brought confirmation of Kendrick Perkins' uselessness within the context of this series. Perkins is a strong, physical, defensive-minded center, perfect for bodying up the likes of Dwight Howard. But against these Mavericks, Perkins lacked the speed to keep up with Tyson Chandler or Dirk Nowitzki.

But even with Perkins playing empty minutes, the Thunder were able to even out the series at 1–1. The first two games were toss-ups, but from this point on the real battle began; the Mavs and Thunder had two chances for exploratory strategy, and after Game 2 it was time for the real adjustments to begin. ■

After scoring 85 points in Game 1 of the Western Conference Finals, Dirk Nowitzki was again on his game in Game 2, shooting 10 of 17 from the field to finish with a game-high 29 points. Unfortunately, Nowitzki's effort was not enough as the Thunder evened the series 1–1.

Game 3

Dallas Mavericks 93
Oklahoma City Thunder 87

Since the Mavs had already had enough practice coming back from fourth quarter deficits, they decided to try a different routine for Game 3. The offense started off hot, though without much help from Dirk Nowitzki. Six Mavericks scored in the opening frame, as crisp passing attacked Oklahoma City's defense so quickly that no rotating Thunder defender could respond. Couple that ball movement with some early defensive pressure, and the Mavs exited the first quarter with a 15-point lead.

From that point, the game was all about lead building and maintenance. DeShawn Stevenson and Shawn Marion made things as difficult as possible for Kevin Durant—an absolute necessity given Nowitzki's strangely poor shooting. Part of a true group defensive effort, Stevenson and Marion did their jobs by contesting as many shots as possible. Durant drifted into a lull, the Thunder offense didn't put Durant in a position to succeed, and Oklahoma City head coach Scott Brooks just watched the whole thing happen.

With Durant shadowed, Russell Westbrook took his cue to be more aggressive. He attacked the basket and went to the foul line 14 times, but his performance overall was a mixed bag; Westbrook finished with 30 points but made just 40 percent of his shots in the process, and he had just four assists to seven turnovers. He forced the issue a bit more than he should have, but the stagnation of the Thunder offense also left him with little choice.

The Maverick lead swelled to as much as 23 points, but Dallas' performance on both ends of the court began to crumble in the fourth quarter. Rather that continue to execute the balanced offense that had created such a substantial advantage, the Mavs began to defer to Nowitzki, and sacrificed several possessions in their attempts to force him the ball. It didn't take long for the Thunder to rally, and though Nowitzki eventually did score enough to preserve the lead, Dallas very nearly blew a huge lead in the postseason for a second time, and almost lost a game that shouldn't have even been competitive in the final minutes.

Though the defensive troubles had more or less been corrected since Games 1 and 2, the Mavs were still in a dogfight. Each of the first three games of the Western Conference Finals were winnable for both teams, and though individual players had displayed their dominance, no team had yet laid claim to the series as a whole. ■

Tyson Chandler hauled in 15 total rebounds—six on the offensive boards—while scoring eight points as Dallas edged Oklahoma City in Game 3 despite an off shooting night from Dirk Nowitzki.

Game 4

Dallas Mavericks 112
Oklahoma City Thunder 105 OT

Sometimes, it just feels like it's meant to be. Basketball games will forever be decided by those who play within the lines, but games like this one will create doubt in that very idea, as if serendipity itself put points on the scoreboard.

The Mavericks trailed by 15 points with just five minutes remaining in the fourth quarter, and the possibility of a comeback seemed remote even for this team. Five minutes isn't much time when it comes down to it, and the tradeoff that teams experience as they force shots prematurely in an effort to conserve that time typically facilitates the loss. It's not just a matter of making up a certain number of points in a limited amount of time, but budgeting possessions in an effort to get as many opportunities as possible.

So off Dallas went, with a victory still in sight, attempting to create high-percentage opportunities in as little time as possible. Fate didn't score the ensuing buckets; Mavericks did. Predictably, Dirk Nowitzki came up huge in the final frame, but Dallas wouldn't have had a chance to compete without help from Oklahoma City. The Thunder committed several idiotic fouls in the Mavericks' backcourt, and that series of foolish mistakes cost the Thunder their shot at a tied series. Eight of the 17 points the Mavs scored in the final five minutes came off of free throws, scoring acts that necessarily rely on defensive errors. Dallas was phenomenal over the final five minutes of regulation, but OKC was actively involved in its own defeat, a willing participant in its own implosion.

While the Mavericks paraded to the free throw line, the Thunder offense completely froze. Dallas threw the kitchen sink at Kevin Durant and Russell Westbrook, and though Nick Collison, Serge Ibaka, and Thabo Sefolosha had been able to dive to the bucket or make open jumpers throughout most of the game, they could offer no release when the Thunder needed it most. The Mavericks ramped up their defense with a mix of man-to-man and match-up zone coverage (both of which relied heavily on the defensive tandem of Jason Kidd and Shawn Marion, who did much of the heavy lifting on that end), and the Thunder's stagnation did the rest of the work.

Once the Mavs were able to force overtime by way of a minor miracle, the extra period continued with both on their pre-existing trajectories. The team with a nearly spotless record in the clutch continued to work the ball to their star in his favored spots on the floor, while the other failed to create any movement in their offense or gain even the slightest advantage against a suffocating defense. The Mavericks outscored the Thunder 28–6 over the game's final 10 minutes to complete the most amazing comeback in franchise history, and cement an all-time great game by the time the final buzzer sounded. ■

Off balance and with Nick Collison's hand in his face, Dirk Nowitzki releases to score two of his game-high 40 points.

Game 5
Dallas Mavericks 100
Oklahoma City Thunder 96

In fitting fashion, Game 5 unfolded much like each of the previous four games; both the Mavericks and Thunder had a legitimate chance of winning, with both clubs pushing one another to new dramatic heights. The resolution ultimately favored the Mavericks, but Game 5's verdict hung in the air with each of Dirk Nowitzki's high-arcing jumpers. Dallas got it done—with Shawn Marion and J.J. Barea this time acting as Nowitzki's scoring complement—but it wasn't easy. It never was with this Thunder team, even with Nowitzki clicking, Russell Westbrook struggling, and Kevin Durant getting little help from the Thunder's offensive system.

Nick Collison helped in that effort. Over the course of the series, Collison had done what he could to limit Nowitzki by denying him the ball, attempting to push him from his spots, and challenging Nowitzki's dribble. Dirk still scored well (he averaged 32.2 points per game for the series), but he had to work for every look he got over the final few games of the series. Collison was by far the Thunder's most effective defender on Nowitzki, and though he couldn't stop Dirk from busting out another 40-point night in Game 4, it's doubtful that anyone really could.

James Harden made a substantial impact, too, by working as a ball-handler in Oklahoma City's half-court offense. Harden's success in the pick-and-roll gave the Mavs fits, and though their match-up zone was able to take some of that success away, Harden's ability to put pressure on the defense with his drives and shooting remained.

But Collison and Harden's contributions—in addition to what Durant and Westbrook were able to provide—never seemed like they were enough. The Thunder were always in need of a few more stops or a few more baskets. The Mavericks were a team of excess in this series; though Dallas and OKC were locked in a dead heat for the entirety of this series, the Mavs were always able to come up with that little something extra. Call it poise, call it experience, or call it whatever you'd like, but the Dallas Mavericks made it through their long, arduous path to the NBA Finals because of their ability to always generate something more.

It wasn't always Nowitzki, either. The Mavericks star may have been brilliant in the clutch throughout the first three rounds of the playoffs, but Jason Kidd, Jason Terry, Shawn Marion, J.J. Barea, and Tyson Chandler each made

Brendan Haywood battles with Oklahoma City's James Harden during Game 5. Haywood scored seven points off the bench and provided tough defense as the Mavericks won to move on to the NBA Finals.

tremendous plays on both sides of the court in critical moments. By necessity, the Mavs had become an incredible example of a true team concept. They didn't have a legitimate superstar to put alongside Nowitzki, but they had an entire rotation filled with reliable talent. Each player was valuable in his own way, and Rick Carlisle handled the rotation masterfully to put his team in a position to win games.

As a result, the Mavs were always competitive—even when facing a 15-point deficit with just five minutes remaining. Dallas was never once daunted by their skilled opponents nor by the magnitude of the games in which they were playing. Every possession of every game was played as if it was meant to be theirs.

Unrelenting execution got Dallas out of the first round, through the defending champs, and past the formidable Thunder. It earned them their second trip to the NBA Finals in franchise history. It gave every member of Maverick Nation the hope of something more to come, and visions of championship celebrations dancing in their heads. The Mavericks didn't yet know who they'd be facing in the NBA Finals, and in a way, it hardly mattered. Dallas would work tirelessly to implement their game on the NBA's biggest stage, and the rest—the opponent, the wins, the final verdict—would decide itself. ■

(opposite) Jason Terry begins to celebrate after sinking one of his two three-pointers. (above) Dirk Nowitzki celebrates after his three-pointer with 1:14 remaining that put the Mavericks ahead for good. Nowitzki scored 26 points.

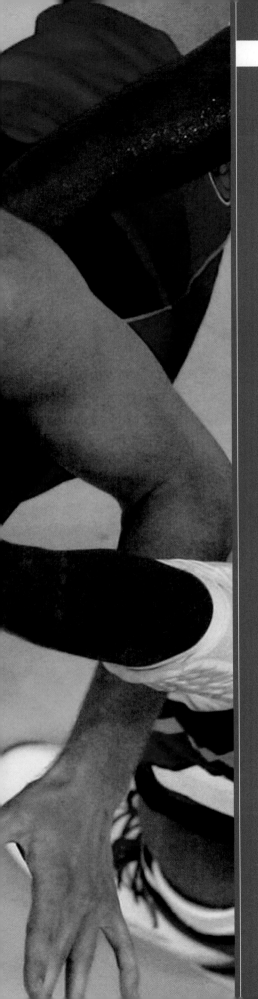

Dirk Nowitzki

Dirk Nowitzki has created a career out of maximizing the success of the theoretically improbable.

The mid-range jumper is, statistically speaking, the least efficient shot in basketball, but Nowitzki has nonetheless been able to carve a hyper-efficient style out of a reliance on that very shot. His attempts are typically accompanied by leans, tilts, and fades, but no contortion can throw off his true shooting stroke; Nowitzki is as accurate as shooters come, despite the incredible degree of difficulty built into most of his shots. There's an odd grace to his jumper, but only one understood in a complete acceptance of Nowitzki's truly unique style. He doesn't soar through the air in super slow motion or have the ball on a string as he dupes opponents with his handle; Nowitzki relies on wondrous footwork, a high release, and the rainbow trajectory of his jumper. There has never been an NBA player quite like Dirk, and while his gaudy scoring totals offer

intrinsic basketball value, Nowitzki is as stylistically significant as any player to ever lace them up.

Whether the Mavs get Nowitzki the ball on the wing, in the post, or at the top of the key, he's capable of putting himself in position for a quality shot. The key is Nowitzki's length; at seven feet tall, Nowitzki is already difficult enough to contest, but when you also factor in his uncommonly high release point and the natural fade on his turnaround jumper, he's essentially unblockable. He does miss from time to time, but his technique and physical gifts minimize the defense as a factor, and make the outcome of every shot primarily a product of Nowitzki's own internal process.

All of which obscures the fact that almost every jumper that Nowitzki takes should be a miss. Probability never favors those who create obstacles for themselves,

Dirk Nowitzki goes up strong in Game 1 of the NBA Finals. Nowitzki scored a game-high 27 points in the loss.

Dirk Now

Dirk Nowitzki looks to pass the ball during the Western Conference Finals. An excellent distributor of the ball, he has a career average of 2.7 assists per game.

and the odd release and one-footed form that Nowitzki typically employs on his fadeaway should only serve to slash his accuracy. Almost inexplicably, it doesn't. Everything about Nowitzki's approach is unconventional, and yet he stands as one of the game's all-time greatest scorers, undisturbed by the fact that he's somehow thrived off of routinely accomplishing the impossible.

The 2010–2011 season was no exception, as Nowitzki completed another successful campaign in a truly remarkable career. Nowitzki has been a Maverick since day one, and his 13-year career in Dallas has largely operated like clockwork; he's averaged more than 21 points per game in every season since 2000, and though his rebounding numbers have dwindled in recent years, his performance on that end has held relatively consistent. Thanks to his impeccable health (this was the first season since his rookie year that Nowitzki played fewer than 76 games) and unfailing jumper, Nowitzki is among the most reliable commodities that the NBA has to offer.

Nowitzki has also sought to address every criticism of his game over the years through a systematic elimination of his weaknesses. When his game was deemed to be too reliant on perimeter shooting, he went to the low block and developed one of the most effective low-

(opposite) A key component to Nowitzki's success is his dedication to practice and conditioning. 2010–2011 marked the first season since Nowitzki's rookie year that he played in less than 76 regular-season games. (above) There's no solution for defending Dirk Nowitzki. Smaller players are beaten inside while bigger players can't keep up with his athleticism.

post games in basketball. When opponents swarmed him with double teams, he learned to adapt by throwing well-timed passes to open teammates. When his defensive limitations became an issue, he developed a strip move that could ward off opponents attacking the rim, and learned to be a quietly successful team defender. Nowitzki may not possess the all-around greatness of LeBron James, but he's a relentless player in search of a complete game. His work ethic is legendary, and through those long hours in the gym (and unorthodox training sessions with his long-time friend and mentor, Holger Geschwindner) Nowitzki has been able to mold himself into a star. The talent and aptitude were there, but Nowitzki flies in the face of probability because of his incredible preparation and unyielding drive.

Those same factors also make Nowitzki one of the greatest clutch performers of his generation. With the game on the line, Nowitzki is one of the best candidates out there to take the final shot; Kobe Bryant, Carmelo Anthony, and Dwyane Wade have their advocates, but Nowitzki has been hitting big shots at a high rate for the better part of a decade. Some confuse the Mavericks various premature playoff exits with an inability in Nowitzki to step up in big moments, but that couldn't be further from the truth. That

(opposite) Nowitzki puts up a jump shot during the Western Conference Finals. (above) Nowitzki reaches up to block the shot of Oklahoma City's Nick Collison. The NBA's MVP in 2007, Nowitzki has averaged one block per game for his career.

clutch pedigree speaks for itself, and his production in the playoffs on the whole somehow exceeds his already sterling regular season marks. Nowitzki is one of just four players in the history of the league to average 25 points and 10 rebounds per game throughout their postseason careers, a distinction from which even Nowitzki's Hall-of-Fame-worthy contemporaries (Shaquille O'Neal, Tim Duncan, Kevin Garnett) are excluded.

Because he is nearly 33 years old, the realities of Nowitzki's age are inescapable. His game will decline at some point—his defensive rotations will be a half-second slower, his drives to the rim a bit less open, and his trips up and down the court even more of a plod than usual. Yet for the foreseeable future, Nowitzki will still be Nowitzki. As his physical limitations close off certain avenues to success, he'll find new ones, just as he's done for the entirety of his career. He hasn't milked his natural athleticism for all it's worth, but created a suitable counterplan reliant on practice and technique. That silky jumper isn't going anywhere, and long after that Finals MVP trophy on his mantle has begun to collect dust, Nowitzki will still be spinning, fading, and dropping 20-plus points a night well into the twilight of his career. ■

(opposite) Driving on Kevin Durant, Dirk Nowitzki shows ball-handling skills that are unique amongst NBA big men. (above) Nowitzki hits a fadeaway in the face of Oklahoma City's Serge Ibaka. Even opposing centers have a hard time contesting Nowitzki's jump shot, thanks to his large frame, long arms, and unique release point high above his head.

Jason Terry

Dirk Nowitzki said it best: Jason Eugene Terry—or "JET," as he's more affectionately known in Dallas—is "a confident young man."

He postures for the crowd, both to pump up fans at the American Airlines Center (with whom Terry shares a special rapport) and antagonize those on the road. He jaws with other players on the court. He gives opposing teams bulletin board material with his bombastic sound bites. He takes tough shots with defenders right in his grill, and drains them.

That said, don't mistake JET's self-belief for arrogance or a sense of entitlement; Terry has actually come off the bench for most of his Mavericks career despite being the team's second-best scorer, an act of deference to the team concept that's rarer in professional basketball than it should be. Terry is, at his core, a true company man, a team player willing to do whatever it is that the Mavs demand of him.

Case in point: in the 2010–2011 season, Terry made significant strides on the defensive end. JET had identified defensive performance as an area for improvement after his off-season talks with the Mavericks coaching staff, and he came into the new season with an entirely revamped defensive energy. Terry's size can make things difficult for him when he's forced to defend bigger guards capable of exploiting their height advantage, but his effort level was never in question; Terry relentlessly chased opponents around screens and pressured the ball beautifully. Dallas needed Terry to improve defensively in order to bolster their overall team defense, and JET answered the call by way of his own motivations.

Jason Terry works against Miami's Jason Williams in the 2006 NBA Finals. After the 2005–2006 season, the Mavericks rewarded Terry with a six-year contract.

Terry is nothing if not sure of himself, but only to a degree that allows him to function well as an NBA player and step up when the Mavs need him most. Terry's clutch résumé is quite illustrious, but the fact that Dallas' late-game offense often begins with the ball in his hands is perhaps the most telling praise of all.

With a game hanging in the balance, Rick Carlisle often puts Terry and Nowitzki in a position to run a pick-and-roll on the right side of the floor, a zone of complete comfort for both players. The dance that unfolds doesn't always result in a made bucket and a victory, but Dallas is virtually guaranteed a quality shot by virtue of Terry's strengths as a ball-handler, shooter, and passer. He's a benevolent combo guard, and his assortment of skills makes him a perfect pick-and-roll partner for Nowitzki.

Together, Terry and Nowitzki have acted as the core of the Mavericks' high-powered offense for seven straight seasons. Nowitzki is unquestionably the brighter star, but Terry's contributions cannot be discounted; JET may not be as efficient as Nowitzki nor as capable of scoring in isolation, but he's a fantastic complementary piece, capable of functioning as an integral part of strong-side play action or waiting along the perimeter for an open three-point attempt. ∎

(opposite) A fan favorite in Dallas, Jason Terry knows how to engage with the fans. His personality complements his tenacious scoring game, making Terry the perfect energy player off the bench. (above) Terry's speed and penchant for coming up with steals has allowed him to make fast-break opportunities a hallmark of his game.

Jason Kidd

In an age where positional norms are being challenged at every turn, Jason Kidd is a remnant of a simpler time. He doesn't score like Russell Westbrook or Derrick Rose, but simply initiates the offense, finds his teammates, and generally acts out the role of the ideal old-school point guard. He'll go down as one of the greatest to ever play the position and, at long last, has erased the only remaining blemish on his NBA career by winning a title.

Kidd's road to the Larry O'Brien trophy spanned 17 seasons, during which Kidd was—at various stages—a rookie phenom, a dynamic athlete, an All-Star, one of the league's top players, an occasional malcontent, and an aging floor general. He's seen the peak of his career come and go, but even at 38 years old Kidd remains a legitimate impact player. He still has the vision to make plays that only a handful of people on the planet can make, and he combines that vision with a pragmatic offensive approach and some staunch defense.

All of that empowers Kidd, but the keystone to his longevity has been the development of a consistent three-point shot. His progression seemed to happen overnight upon his return to Dallas; Kidd shot 46 percent during his first partial season after re-joining the Mavs, despite never topping 36 percent during his seven seasons in New Jersey. In three seasons and change, Kidd has settled in at 39 percent from beyond the arc during his second tour with the Mavs, an evolution that has helped Kidd become a true perimeter player.

Earlier in Kidd's career, the strengths of his game were reliant on the drive. He used his speed and athleticism to put defenses in compromising

After 14 straight playoff appearances, Jason Kidd won his first career NBA championship with the Mavericks in 2010–2011. Kidd, who was originally selected by Dallas as the No. 2 pick in the 1994 draft, rejoined the Mavericks in 2008.

positions, and then punished them with a perfectly threaded pass to an open teammate. With that athleticism gone and Kidd's feet heavy, that approach was no longer an option. So Kidd finds cutters while positioned at the three-point arc, ready and willing to fire up a shot if the ball swings back his way.

Without that ability to compensate for the limitations of his age, the Mavs—and Kidd—would not be NBA champions. The development of one specific skill may seem like such a minor aspect of convoluted game with myriad variables, but Kidd's ability to trigger the offense without acting as a liability pushed the Mavs over the top. Not only did Dallas have another shooter on the floor, but one willing to make the extra swing pass and act as a conduit for impromptu offense.

Plus, even though he no longer has the speed to keep up with lightning-quick point guards, Kidd's savvy has made him the Mavs' most versatile defender. Over the course of Dallas' playoff run, Kidd defended Andre Miller, Brandon Roy, Kobe Bryant, Kevin Durant, Russell Westbrook, LeBron James, and Dwyane Wade. He draws a tough assignment at every turn, and regardless of his opponents' size or skills, he manages to get the job done. ∎

(opposite) One of the best point guards in NBA history, Jason Kidd has been steadily working on his Hall of Fame résumé. (above) Jason Kidd adjusted to the realities of age by improving his shooting touch. Kidd has shot over 40 percent from long range three times in his career, all since rejoining the Mavericks during the 2007–2008 season.

Tyson Chandler

The Dallas Mavericks have long been led by committee. Dirk Nowitzki will forever lead by example, with his unbelievable performances and efficient shooting dictating a certain expectation for his teammates. Jason Kidd is a leader through experience, a veteran floor general who knows the ins and outs of an offense as well as any player in the NBA. Jason Terry is a motivator and an X-factor, capable of pushing the Mavs to new heights. And somewhere in that equation is Tyson Chandler, who quickly became Dallas' emotional leader despite playing but a single year in a Mavericks uniform.

Chandler simply has a presence and style that command immediate attention. For better or worse, Chandler is a player dictated by passion. He plays all-out for every second he's on the court, and while that approach results in defensive excellence and fantastic offensive rebounding, it also tends to get him in foul trouble. Still, that approach is endearing for teammates playing alongside Chandler throughout the slog of the regular season. As Chandler beats his chest with his fist following a big play, the Mavericks hear only a war drum and go forth to do battle alongside a center who will never relent.

The Mavs' defense has thus gained from more than just Chandler's length or ability to defend the pick-and-roll. He acts as a manifestation of the team's rally, an embodiment of the tenacious execution that Dallas

After jumping to the NBA out of high school as a raw prospect, Tyson Chandler has refined his game over 10 seasons to become one of the league's most tenacious and athletic big men.

hopes to enact on every defensive possession. Chandler's energy is contagious, and though Maverick centers of the recent past have had their defensive strengths, none has championed defensive fervor like Chandler.

Plus, Chandler's offensive impact is often underrated. It's true that Chandler's ability to create shots is limited (he has neither a low-post game nor a consistent jumper, and thus isn't a valid go-to option on offense), but Dallas was the best offensive team in the league with Chandler on the floor this season. His ability to hit the offensive glass helps, but even more beneficial were Chandler's screens and rolls, both of which assist in the Mavericks' all-important spacing. Chandler is such a powerful finisher on the pick-and-roll that teams have to account for him charging down the lane, and often leave another Maverick open in the process. In the case that opposing defenders elect not to rotate over to defend Chandler in such a scenario, then the rest of the Mavs immediately look to set him up with an alley-oop dunk.

Within the context of this fluid, high-powered offense, that's all Chandler really needs to do. The Mavs have their post-up threat. They have shooters from the outside. All that's required of Chandler is that he screen hard and flash to the basket to create a position of instant advantage for one Maverick or another. ■

(opposite) Rick Carlisle has tapped into Tyson Chandler's talents more effectively than any of the coaches Chandler has played for over 10 NBA seasons with four teams. Carlisle counts on Chandler to provide tough defense and play to his strengths on offense. (above) With an ability to produce highlight-reel dunks, Chandler can be a force on the offensive end. His average of 10.1 points per game in 2010–2011 was the second-highest scoring average of his career.

Shawn Marion

Shawn Marion doesn't do "the little things," or "fill in the gaps," in the Mavericks' performance. He simply does things that no other Maverick can do. No one else on Dallas' roster packs Marion's combination of effective defense, solid rebounding, and versatile slashing offense, and that unique package of skills made him an absolutely essential (and adaptable) element in the Mavs' championship run.

There's no question that Marion benefits from playing alongside players like Dirk Nowitzki and Jason Kidd, but Marion deserves credit for his ability to create mismatches. Dallas may not feed Marion on offense as deliberately as they do Nowitzki, but Marion has nonetheless shown the ability to attack defenders big and small. Marion's array of unorthodox runners makes him oddly effective when facing up from the mid-post or cutting through the paint, and his ability to hit a right-handed hook after backing down an undersized opponent creates high-percentage looks for the Dallas offense. When opposing teams overload on Nowitzki or Jason Terry, it's Marion who acts to relieve the offensive pressure, a skill that grew even more valuable after Caron Butler was lost for the season to a knee injury.

Reaching up to throw down a dunk, Shawn Marion still has plenty of the explosiveness that earned him the nickname "The Matrix" before he had even played an NBA game. A unique combination of size and athleticism, his athletic offensive game has caused trouble for defenders throughout his career.

As effective as Marion was on offense, his role as wing stopper in tandem with Jason Kidd gave the Mavs an incredible luxury. Together, Marion and Kidd were able to make things just difficult enough for Kevin Durant and Russell Westbrook in the Western Conference Finals, and later, just difficult enough for LeBron James and Dwyane Wade in the NBA Finals. Marion may not be the physical specimen he once was, but he still has good technique, great length, and a reluctance to leave his feet. He's not duped by pump fakes, and simply tries to maintain the best position possible to get a hand in the face of an opposing star.

Every component of a championship team is important—there's too little room for error in the NBA playoffs for any element to be discounted—but Marion was perhaps the most unheralded. He didn't outscore Nowitzki, pump up the crowd like Terry, or anchor the defense like Chandler. He just did everything he could to push the Mavericks as far as they could go, and while some may not appreciate Marion's versatility for the weapon that it is, we know better. ∎

(opposite) A four-time All-Star, Shawn Marion's strength and size allows several positions and defend nearly any opponent. During the NBA Finals, Marion first shut down Dwayne Wade, then slowed LeBron James enough to help the Mavericks win the title. (above) Marion has averaged 20 or more points in a season twice in his career and is still a key contributor to the Mavericks' offense.

Rick Carlisle

National Basketball Association coaches, even more so than players, are defined by their ability or inability to win championships. It's for that reason that Rick Carlisle, a fantastic Xs and Os coach, was able to fly under the radar for so long.

Consider this championship run his coming out party. He managed to negate all of the potential mismatches that the Portland Trailblazers held in the first round. He out-coached Phil Jackson—considered by many to be the greatest NBA coach of all-time—in four consecutive games to sweep the defending champions. He found new and exciting ways to get the ball to Dirk Nowitzki in the Western Conference Finals, while holding Kevin Durant and Russell Westbrook to acceptable levels of production. He empowered J.J. Barea to attack from the high pick-and-roll, and had the foresight to insert Barea into the starting lineup in the NBA Finals. Every clipboard he touched turned to gold.

Carlisle will be the first to tell you that all of this means nothing without players executing and defending, but there's still something to be said about the value of a coach putting his players in a position to succeed. Carlisle ran a coaching clinic in the playoffs, primarily by balancing a commitment to his established strategy with the ingenuity to introduce new wrinkles. There were no drastic overhauls, merely subtle shifts in approach. Those shifts paid off big time, and Carlisle has emerged from the postseason looking like the smartest guy in the room.

A look back at Carlisle's coaching history shows that this is nothing really new, but the stars finally aligned for Carlisle and the Mavs. Carlisle continued to prepare well and devise excellent game plans. The roster was finally filled with the kind of balance on which Carlisle's system thrives. And—most importantly—Dallas subscribed to the belief that they were a team worthy of the NBA Finals, and executed as such ■

Rick Carlisle has won more than 700 games as a head coach over nine NBA seasons.

Mark Cuban

An NBA team is only as good as its ownership, and since Mark Cuban purchased the Mavs in 2000, they've been among the top teams in the league. That should tell you all you need to know about the personnel Cuban has put in power, the players he's invested in over the years, and his own willingness to foot the bill for success. The Mavericks were lucky to find a true superstar in Dirk Nowitzki, but identifying and grooming talent is only part of building a winning team. Beyond that, ownership has to be willing to pay for quality supporting players and coaches, and trust the right general managers to run the show.

Cuban accomplished all of that and more, and while his activity within the team and controversial quotes have made him into a polarizing figure (and a character of sorts) in professional sports, behind the loud-mouthed instigator seen on TV is an owner who has kept his team competitive for 11 straight seasons. No one can doubt Cuban's commitment to his team; his ownership has always been more than merely a business venture, and he's among the rare breed of owners criticized for perhaps caring too much. The result of that is an outspoken fan functioning as the spokesman of the franchise, but also a dedicated financier willing to invest considerable coin for the betterment of the team.

The luxury tax line acts as a functional hard cap for many NBA owners,

Despite a penchant for the outrageous and controversial, Mark Cuban has proven to be an owner thoroughly dedicated to making the Mavericks a winning organization.

but Cuban has no qualms about going over and beyond it in his efforts to improve the roster. Not many owners would be willing to pay both Tyson Chandler and Brendan Haywood a starting center's salary, but Cuban signed the checks and both players were crucial to Dallas' playoff run. That same willingness to spend occasionally has led to some curious signings, but Cuban has been able to minimize his (and president of basketball operations Donnie Nelson's) mistakes by taking on those of others in exchange. That may not sound beneficial, but consider this example: Cuban and Nelson were able to trade the overpaid Raef LaFrentz to the Boston Celtics for even more overpaid Antoine Walker, and though Walker was hardly a prize, Dallas was able to flip him to the Atlanta Hawks in the following off-season for eventual franchise mainstay Jason Terry. All general managers and owners make mistakes, but the ability to rectify those mistakes by working to the full extent of financial flexibility that the collective bargaining agreement allows is priceless.

Thus is the story of Mark Cuban's Mavericks. Every decision made along the way wasn't perfect, but Cuban's passion for his team kept the motor going. Dallas stalled with various misguided acquisitions, but the willingness to do whatever it took to move forward was always there. ■

(opposite) Mark Cuban celebrates the Mavericks' 2011 Western Conference championship. Both of Dallas' NBA Finals appearances have come since Cuban purchased the franchise. (above) Cuban shoots around at the American Airlines Center.

A self-made million-aire who first came to Dallas in 1982, Mark Cuban spends more time interacting with fans than any other NBA owner.